TEENAGERS
A Family Survival Guide

D0522561

By the same author

A Marriage Survival Guide
Getting It Right
Generation Games
The British Abroad
A Parents' Survival Guide

fiction
The Man for the Job

TEENAGERS
A Family Survival Guide

LAURIE GRAHAM

Chatto & Windus
LONDON

Published in 1992 by
Chatto & Windus Ltd
20 Vauxhall Bridge Road
London SW1V 2SA

All rights reserved. No part of this publication may
be reproduced, stored in a retrieval system, or transmitted
in any form, or by any means, electronic, mechanical, photocopying,
recording or otherwise, without the prior permission
of the publisher.

A CIP catalogue record for this book is
available from the British Library.

ISBN 0 7011 3842 4

Copyright © Laurie Graham 1992
Illustrations © Karen Donnelly 1992

Laurie Graham has asserted her right to be
identified as the author of this work

Phototypeset by Intype, London
Printed in Great Britain by
Mackays of Chatham plc,
Chatham, Kent

Contents

Introduction

A few years ago, when I was a veteran of sleepless nights and matted shoulders, I wrote about my experience of raising four small children and I was delighted to find that I struck a chord with many of my readers. There was no shortage of books on parenthood, but the need I had felt, for something that conveyed what a grisly, sticky, wonderful experience parenthood could be, was hardly being met. So I wrote my first *Parents' Survival Guide*, not realising that I was about to fall into yet another black hole of angst, debt and euphoria – my four children were about to become teenagers.

I read a few books, but by then I knew the form. It is fine and interesting to read about the physiology, and the psychology of adolescence, and to become acquainted with the laws your children may transgress. But what I still longed to know was how it *feels* to live with creeping redundancy and a baby who suddenly needs to shave. Very few books even attempted to tell me about that.

I turned to my friends and neighbours. Many of them were further down the road of parenting teenagers than I was, and they were happy and relieved to tell me everything they knew. While they talked, I wrote, but always with one eye on my own evolving domestic scene. At times, as my own children discovered a world of gigs and sex and designer jeans, when hurricane force crises caught me midships, the writing came to a halt.

As I completed the final draft of this book my oldest teenager reached the age of eighteen and left home. In the excitement and sadness of the occasion I thought I caught a whiff of something new, a hint of more tranquil times ahead, and the pleasures of having grown-up children. But for now I am still inescapably in the thick of Teenagers – not the book, not the movie – just The Experience.

This book is dedicated to my teenage children, and to the dozens of other parents who were generous enough to level with me.

LAURIE GRAHAM

Ten Essential Things for the Parent of Teenagers to Have

A telephone lock

A working knowledge of quadratic equations and the history of the League of Nations

Eyes in the back of your head

A willingness to close them

A supply of Industrial Strength Clearasil

A photograph of yourself, aged fifteen

A pen that writes, attached by heavy steel links to a large immovable object

A friend with wonderful grown-up children

A pair of unladdered tights whose whereabouts is known only to you and God

A life of your own

Ten Useful Things for a Teenager to Know

Peroxide followed by semi-permanent black can equal green hair

Green hair followed by burgundy dye can lead to no hair at all

Richard Branson didn't get A levels

Neither did the girl who clears tables at the Berni

There is a right way and a wrong way with batteries

In 1964 your mother used to iron her hair

1 a.m. is not a few minutes after 11 p.m. It's 120 minutes

So far there is no evidence that crossed fingers are effective as contraceptives

The Electricity Board can't tell the difference between the heater you meant to turn off and the one you just left on all day

Free love and rebellion were invented by your Dad, and that's official

1 *The Long Goodbye*
Modern Western adolescence

So you're expecting a teenager? How wonderful. During the thirteen-year wait some of the excitement does wear off, but the fact remains that you are embarking on one of the most exhilarating rides human relations can provide. You are on the brink of a time when night will be turned into day and the house will be cluttered with the hardware of adolescence, a time of physical stress and emotional strain, awash in a sea of sex hormones. A time when your telephone bill will treble.

You can never be sure when a teenager is going to arrive. The gestation period varies widely and unpredictably, even within the same family. Some people are still pink and innocent at sixteen. Some have Woodbine Breath at thirteen. Some go to bed one night with a Pony Club annual and a mug of cocoa, and emerge the next morning with three earrings and a bad attitude. No one heard a thing. While the world slept, a horrible metamorphosis took place beneath the duvet, and there it is, a physiological near-miss in designer denim.

But your teenager may not arrive in this way. The phased entrance is a popular alternative. With this option, the physical manifestations and the stroppy mind-set arrive on different days, and not in any particular order. This makes it possible to accommodate rebellion before acne sets in, or vice versa. If this sounds like a more attractive proposition, don't get excited. It is all beyond your control. The genetic template that makes each human being unique will decide whether your teenager arrives on the first Thursday in January, or weekly throughout 1994.

What we can say with certainty is that some time between the age of twelve and twenty a teenager is born. It is not a modern aberration that you can escape by taking your family to live on a tiny island in the Pacific. Teenagers in grass skirts may be better understood and better catered for than teenagers in central Milton Keynes, but they are teenagers for all that. It is not a stage of life that can be skipped, no matter how sensible or biddable or angelic the child. Even Mother Teresa was spotty and misunderstood for a year or two.

It may not be possible to predict when your teenager will make his entrance, but with foresight it is possible to determine where you will be in your life when it happens. Teenage parents themselves become the parents of teenagers in their early thirties. This has always been promulgated as a point in favour of being a young parent, on the basis that at thirty-four you still remember what it felt like to be fourteen and will deal with problems sympathetically.

This is a myth. And it is a myth made more annoying for being based on the faulty premiss that what you can recall at thirty-four you will have forgotten by fifty. No one ever forgets their own teens.

The myth is that our own recollections have much relevance. There is nothing new under the sun, it is true. But the main point of adolescence, the very *raison d'être* of teenagers, is to differ, and mainly to differ from their parents. A vital part of deciding who you are is deciding who you're not. And your Mum and Dad have to be top of the list. You probably look like them. Sometimes you accidentally sound like them. And they are in possession of some seriously worrying information about you, like how you used to love 'Nelly the Elephant'. Teenagers need to put distance between the young adult they are inventing, and their former selves, with all those embarrassing, sentimental hangers-on. They definitely do not want to hear that when you were fourteen, which seems like only yesterday, *exactly* the same thing happened to you.

In a sense, the further you advance into the decrepitude of middle age, the easier it becomes for your teenager to define himself as different. On the other hand, teenagers who are preoccupied with appearances do not like their parents to be mistaken for their grandparents. They are able to take quiet pleasure in having parents who still have a spring in their step, just as long as there is no question of competition. When a mother and daughter are mistaken for sisters, it's the mother who's thrilled.

The best age to be the parent of a teenager is when you've

decided, or almost decided, who you are, and are still in robust enough health to enjoy it. When you can remember with agonising clarity what it felt like to be gangling and gauche, but have the humility not to talk about it. When you've learned the difference between personal standards and crimes against humanity, and are ready to relinquish the idea that you are the only thing standing between civilised behaviour and the end of the world. The arrival of your first teenager is a very good time to back off, calm down and lighten up.

You may have other children you feel you should prepare for the shape of things to come. But there's a problem. What *is* the shape of things to come? And what is its estimated time of arrival? There aren't many certainties with teenagers. One of the few is that they do not make good room-mates for younger siblings. Nor for older ones. In fact they make completely impossible room-mates for any member of the human race, and should therefore be housed separately, preferably in soundproofed seclusion.

If the smallness of the house or the size of your family makes this impossible you had better get used to the idea that blood will be shed. A curtained alcove is better than nothing, and it is also better than a nice big bedroom that has to be shared with the owner of the definitive My Little Pony collection. One of the most precious things you can give your teenager is her own door to slam. Think of it as a gift to the family.

You can also issue a Turbulence Warning. 'Some time in the next two years your brother is going to be touchy, reclusive, noisy, silent, stunningly mature, bristly, and foolhardy.' Does it help? I don't think so. You really have to wait for the first bump and then explain the situation to the tearful eight-year-old who had the misfortune to get in the way. 'I know Nick always let you go under his bed to search for tennis balls, but Nick has grown up now, so under his bed is private.'

It can be hard for a younger member of the family. Yesterday he had a friend. Now the friend is a snarling stranger who locks the bathroom door. But if an eight-year-old, or even a five-year-old can grasp concepts like PRIVATE, a fourteen-year-old can certainly grasp the idea that he shouldn't leave his path to adulthood littered with casualties. It is sometimes possible to touch something gentle in a spiky teenager by reminding him that his little brother thinks he's God Almighty.

Having more than one baby in the house at the same time is something parents have thrust upon them. No one would knowingly volunteer for a multiple birth unless it was absolutely their only chance of parenthood. When twins or more happen, parents steel themselves for a major assault on their energy and their bank balance, smile, and do the best they can. But when parents are building a family, child by carefully planned child, few of them think about the shape of that family fifteen years on when it will contain a multiplicity of teenagers. They figure that having a seventeen-year-old at the same time as a fifteen-year-old and a thirteen-year-old won't be any problem and could even be fun because they'll just love to borrow each other's clothes and stay up half the night playing records. Then one day, when they've prised the seventeen-year-old's fingers from around the scrawny neck of the thirteen-year-old, and issued everyone with their very own colour-coded, monogrammed leg-shaving equipment, they realise. Too late.

One teenager at a time is a challenge. Two at a time is a tightrope walk. With three or more teenagers there is an exponential leap in the amount of trouble in your life. Each teenager is a quick-change artist, a deep and ominously rumbling enigma. And none of them is self-contained. An eruption in one may trigger a firework display from another, and the kind of agreement I always feel children should have amongst themselves – to take turns at playing up – don't always work out. Sometimes you are bound to get stereophonic mayhem.

Even if you only have one in-house teenager, you automatically qualify for close contact with others in a sort of surrogate capacity. Other people's teenagers will eat your food, use your telephone to argue with their parents, sleep on your floor, claim to have been sleeping on your floor when they weren't, and block your lavatory.

Teenagers prefer to travel in packs. There is little sense in fighting this tendency, and actually it's quite a good system. Most packs are ostentatious but harmless. They are the perfect forum for experimentation and self-invention. When you want to be different the safest way to do it is with five other people who'd like to be exactly the same kind of different.

The adolescent who never joins a tribe excites admiration in parents, especially other people's parents. They rather wish *their* daughter would stay at home and practise arpeggios instead of trying to liberate boys from their boxer shorts. And sometimes those who resist pack life do emerge as strong, socially adept young adults, with a well-defined sense of self. But very often they don't. Teenage oddballs tend to turn into adult oddballs. There's almost nothing you can do about it. If your oddball is an Einstein kind of oddball, look on in awe. Wait for history to be made. But if he's just odd – not musical, not inventive, not training for the 1996 Olympics, just brooding in his room, picking his nose, and reading *Firearms Monthly* – it wouldn't hurt to nudge him in the direction of a pack. There is something about a few years of wearing identical sweatshirts and talking in the same silly voices that is apparently good for future mental health.

So for a time other people's teenagers will become part of your extended family, and your children will likewise graft themselves on to other households. When they were small they had other children in to play, occasionally to tea, and very occasionally to sleep. Teenagers don't come to play. They come for mid-evening snacks involving two loaves of bread. They come at 5 p.m. on Friday to prepare for a party at 9 p.m. on Saturday. And they come to sleep. For a week. A month. Who's counting?

Some household features act like magnets. A pool table will bring every teenager within a five-mile radius to your doorstep. Any kind of self-contained accommodation – a separate sitting room, a separate telephone – will have them piling in, and any room painted black or lined with old egg cartons, any hint of coloured light bulbs, guarantees you a two-star entry (at least) in the next edition of the Good Hangout Guide.

Maybe you don't want to be in the Good Hangout Guide? It's easily avoided. But you really need to decide one way or the other before your first teenager gets up to speed. Once you've gained a reputation for being hospitably cool dudes, it is difficult to shake it off. If you're not sure, far better to start with tense formality, shaking hands with newcomers *after* they've removed their Doc Martens, and insisting that your son keeps his Yogi Bear eiderdown until it's worn out. You can always relax a little, later. Once the word has gone round that you're not the kind of parents to be messed with.

On the whole I'm in favour of other people's teenagers. They have the twin assets of being a vital source of information on what your own children are up to, whilst saving all their worst behaviour for their own parents. Woo them with pizza. Take them into your confidence. If you have a teenager who's heading for trouble, her friends will be the first to know. Play your cards right and you could be next.

When your children are tiny and you are juggling nursery places and mortgage repayments and promotion opportunities and the vexed question of whose turn it was to buy toilet paper, you look forward to the day when you won't need to be in so many places at once. You dream of your children being able to come home from school all by themselves. And sometimes you even fantasise about coming home yourself, tired from a late meeting and frozen points at Burgess Hill, to a warm industrious kitchen scene, school work on the table, and dinner in the oven. Dream on.

Your teenagers may not need you to be waiting at the school gate, but there are a thousand places they will still need you, however grudgingly. This is not the time when you can be available for foreign assignments or romantic holidays for two. That time, if it ever passes your way again, will have to be squeezed between your last teenager leaving home and your début as a caring, sharing grandparent, or nurse to an ageing parent.

Teenagers need you to be silent and invisible, but very palpably *there*. Not so much for the little practicalities, like food, and clean clothes, although they'll let you, if you insist. What they really need you to be is a reference point. You, with your spreading waistline and your Fairport Convention albums, are a marker on their path of self-invention. You are the standard-bearer, the wall of resistance for them to kick, and sometimes to lean against. You have to be there, refusing to take responsibility, before they'll believe they have to take responsibility for themselves. Without your baggy cardigan their slashed denim would shrivel to insignificance. You are a powerful, negative source of creativity. You are their Absolute Zero.

They need you around too because their crises can be very big ones. They may have to make decisions of life and death. Or they may have a brush with the law. Your role as slayer of dragons and fixer of messes should diminish as your children reach their late teens. But it is an invariable rule of parenthood that a child who is going to crash his moped will not do it until you're away having a quiet weekend in the Cotswolds. With teenage children you have all the sensations of redundancy, without the freedom or the big cheque.

But is there anything to look forward to? Certainly. Unless you're an incurable Control Freak. Teenagers lead fast-moving complicated lives. They're very interesting to observe. If you enjoyed reading her *Wind in the Willows*, just wait till she discovers William Burroughs. If it was exciting to see her master tying her shoelaces, imagine her being able to help you with positrons and quarks. And if you are the person who shovelled in the mashed banana and helped him make pastry worms, prepare to stand back in amazement while he cooks dinner for the girl of his dreams.

'How are your children?' is a question you don't mind when you can frame your answer around chicken-pox and swimming certificates. Later on, when there's nothing much to report except purple hair, you can feel beleaguered. Every one else's children seem to be clean-cut dead certs for Oxford University. Other parents won't always tell you the truth, unless you see enough of their teenagers to have a pretty good idea anyway. Some families play out desperate games of pretence. They cling to pieces of wreckage and say 'Sam's still set on Archaeology. He's just taking a year or two to get this steel band thing out of his system.'

The truth is that all teenagers create turbulence in their families. Even the ones with perfect teeth. Everything changes, parents and children, and often not in step with one another. There's no going back. Only the opportunity to get smarter. And usually, when it's all over, you get what you originally ordered – someone quite separate from you, but closely related, who might win a Nobel Peace prize, or marry someone terrible from Potters Bar, and whatever, you'd trust them with your life.

Or did you hope he'd have a shiny face and be in bed by eight *for ever*?

2 *A Perfectly Normal Teenager*
Teenage hallmarks

If you've got a teenager who is loud, moody, distant and rebellious it won't make your life any more comfortable to know that this is normal, but it may at least put your mind at rest that you haven't gone badly wrong somewhere. The processes that a teenager goes through, physical and emotional, are unavoidable if she is ever to reach maturity.

There are no short cuts, no cryogenic miracles that will suspend her in ice between the ages of thirteen and twenty.

And in terms of her psychological development, it does appear that the more you try to hijack it, or delay it, or mould it in your very own image, the bigger the problems will be, especially for your child. If you don't allow her to grow up at the right time, she'll keep making dispirited efforts to do it for the rest of her life. Or she'll give up, and knowing that she's been thwarted in a vital piece of her development she'll stay chronically angry with her parents, and chronically depressed with herself. We all know people who'd be much healthier now if they hadn't been required to be so bloody perfect thirty years ago.

At one and the same time a teenager is pulled back towards her childhood, with pangs of dependence, and onward to adulthood, with a longing for independence from her parents and her history. Leaving aside what havoc her sex hormones may be wreaking, it's hardly surprising if her moods swing wildly from one extreme to another.

The hallmarks of teenage moods are noisy exuberance or silence, with a face like thunder. When she's on an upward swing she bursts with restless energy. She needs to clatter and fidget around, she needs her music to be on the loud side of loud, and she needs to talk in a silly voice. Silly voices are a vital part of teenage culture. They may be caricatures of hapless schoolteachers, or they may be original creations. Either way they are a very effective way of separating those in the know from the uninitiated. Whole mealtimes may pass without a single intelligible word being said. And sometimes long, expensive phone calls too.

I don't know what teenagers did before telephones. I suppose carrier pigeons flapped back and forth in a cloud of dust and feathers, or arrows with messages wrapped around them hummed across the village green. They must have managed to stay in touch somehow. Now they don't even have the strain of dialling. They can commit the numbers of their dearest friends to the telephone's memory, so that all they need do, when they haven't spoken to anyone for three-quarters of an hour, is lift one finger and let technology make the connections.

Teenage telephone conversations are important, but they are never about anything important. They are just about staying in touch. A system of jungle drums would achieve the same effect at a fraction of the cost. It baffles parents when a teenager dashes to telephone someone she just sat next to on the school bus. What can they possibly have to say? Things like 'What are you doing?' 'Nothing much. How about you?' 'Nothing much. What are you doing later?' 'Dunno. How about you?' 'Dunno. I might phone you.' Variations around this theme can keep your telephone line busy for hours. You start getting letters from friends who don't usually write letters, because they can't get through on the phone. If you want to reduce your phone bill without depriving your teenager of succour and comfort, let her invite her friends round to talk in silly voices instead.

On the downward swing teenagers need solitude. They need to spend long hours mooching, dreaming and gazing into space. Sometimes they need to lie completely inert beneath their duvet. This drives brisk and breezy parents round the bend. Why doesn't she go for a bike ride, why doesn't he put his *Wisdens* in chronological order? They don't, because they actually need time to ponder and fantasise. Hundreds of exciting and frightening possibilities open up before a teenager. She can't sample them all. But she can play around with the idea of them. She can try herself out in a dozen different roles without taking any risks. And she can escape from aspects of her life that she's finding painful. Such as the fact that her parents, whom she does love, are too gruesome for words.

So a normal teenager needs to belong, in particular to a group of other teenagers, and she needs to be separate, mainly from her parents. She needs to be able to let off steam, play, argue, and confirm in as many noisy ways as possible that she is alive. And she needs to withdraw, to her room, or to some inner territory where her parents can never go.

Her parents, who have spent her first fourteen years fixing her up in one way or another, don't know what to do any more. If they nag her she snarls. If they get too chummy she runs a mile. She is in transit, between a way of life her parents chose for her, and a life she has to choose for herself, perhaps even at the risk of breaking her parents' hearts. They are in transit too, from being providers and carers to being respectful spectators. But after years of wiping her nose and bandaging her knee it's hard to stand idly by. Parents desperately want to do something, preferably the right thing. What they have to realise is that during normal teenage development the right place for parents to be is in the wrong.

3 *Suddenly, Last Thursday*
The Physical changes

Once upon a time you had a lithe and nimble little child, with a winning dimpled smile, and skin that was inviting to the touch. Then, one night, the Growing-Up Fairy dropped by and began her work. By morning everything was on the move. Feet and hands, nose and chin, trunk and limbs, were growing before your very eyes. But not all at the same rate. Beneath the skin a great primeval convulsion of fat and muscle was taking place. And above, translucence and downy softness had given way to bristles and pores that winked at you. You no longer had a child who could sit on your lap. You had a child whose lap you could sit on. The question is, would you want to?

Teenagers spend a lot of time peering into the mirror, and no wonder. Nothing looks right any more. Important bits don't seem to match other important bits, and the thought crosses every teenage mind that in one respect or another they belong in a freak show.

When a boy becomes a man his chest and shoulders broaden, his voice deepens, and he grows muscles and body hair. But before this vision of manliness appears there is a time when what you see is a child with enormous hands and feet. He bursts out of his size nines, and his fingers seem too big for his brain. Growing lads can be very bad news around a Crown Derby dinner service.

Then his arms and legs start to catch up with his hands and feet. You might expect this to improve the aesthetic effect, but it doesn't, because his trunk size is still lagging behind. For a while he just looks like a daddy-long-legs with a huge Adam's apple. Boys who are at the arms and legs stage of development are incompatible with standard armchairs and sofas. Their legs dangle over the sides and ends of all normal domestic furniture. And it isn't just the extra yardage and the poor co-ordination. There's something else. Teenage restlessness.

The teenage body is either supine, catatonic, and attached to a personal stereo, or it is in perpetual motion. It flails and fidgets without any obvious stimulus, and its gorilla arms are drawn magnetically towards delicate pieces of Venetian glass.

The more space you can give a teenage boy the less damage there will be.

Of course some parents don't have this problem. Their teenager just doesn't grow, and then they may have a different problem. One very short teenager in a sea of gangling giraffe necks can feel literally out of it. He may not even be able to make himself heard. Teenagers with short parents understand that they're not going to make six feet. They may curse their inheritance, but having grown up with small adults who are in perfect working order they also understand that they're not doomed to a life of hopelessness. A teenager who might expect to grow taller but doesn't will have a harder time of it. Somehow or other he has to compensate. If he chooses the path of bumptiousness he will become a very difficult little man to get along with. If you can do anything to encourage him towards developing his sense of humour instead, the world will have reason to be grateful to you for many years to come.

Girls grow too, of course, and for a while, around the age of twelve or thirteen they outstrip the boys. They look like young women, while the lads still look like little squirts. But the kind of growth that mainly interests a teenage girl is her burgeoning contours. Where a boy lays down muscle, she lays down fat, and very often she won't like how it looks. Sometimes her dislike of how it looks will override every other concern in her life. And if that happens, at best she will become boring, at worst she may be heading for trouble. One of the finest gifts parents can give a teenage girl is the idea that she can live in peace with her body.

The assault on a girl's body image now starts before her teens. At an age when girls' magazines used to carry stories of boarding school japes, they now carry fashion features with photographs of greyhound-thin models. And at an age when

girls used to talk about netball and teachers, and eventually
about boys, they now talk about dieting and boys. Weight
loss is a staple of female small talk these days. And not just
between teenagers. Their mothers, women who are old enough
to know better, are obsessive dieters. They are either just
about to start on yet another new regime, or they are tri-
umphant because they've managed to live on nothing but
grapefruit and cottage cheese for a fortnight. We have an
epidemic of eating disorders amongst teenage girls today, and
it is fuelled, in part at least, by the silly behaviour of their
mothers.

There is only one satisfactory diet for people who are in
good health and who have enough money to buy food, and
that is a diet of variety, balance and moderation. If it can be
shared with others, and if eating can be a social and sensual
celebration, so much the better. I would personally like to see
all pocket calorie counters, bathroom scales and containers of
banana-flavoured meal-substitute gunk banned from households where children are growing up. Mothers are the principal shoppers, cooks and dieters. They are also powerful role
models. However much a teenage girl may distance herself
from images of her mother, she does understand on some
basic level that one day she'll become Mother. It is damaging
and demoralising for her to learn that Mother is constantly
at war with her own body.

A girl usually decides to become anorexic because she
knows her family will buy it. The more of a big deal diet is
in a family the more power an anorexic gains from her
behaviour. And once you've agreed to join battle with her, it
is very difficult to disengage.

Anorexia involves a dramatic weight loss, with a warped
perception of self-image. A girl may have lost 20 per cent or

more of her normal body weight and still complain that she is hideously obese. She may go through the motions of agreeing that she needs to eat more sensibly and at the same time go to elaborate lengths not to do it. Secrecy and denial become weapons in her determination to stay anorexic. And what started as the simple desire to look like the girls in the magazines can become an obsession that is more about control and independence than it is about body weight. Bulimia takes the same obsession to even greater depths of despair. In bulimia, compulsive over-eating alternates with self-induced vomiting, and frantic purging. Both are desperate expressions of self-loathing.

There is no certain protection against these eating disorders. The best parents can do is to provide a home in which there isn't any incentive to fight about food. Some families start these battles with the first spoonful of sieved carrots. A nice clean plate becomes equated with goodness. Messing around with your food becomes a capital offence. And the arbiter of these standards is the woman who lugged the stuff home from the supermarket, peeled it, sliced it, slaved over a hot stove and generally laid down her life that others might eat. Mum.

It is one thing to take care and pleasure in feeding a family well. If it weren't for women most families would live on fried egg sandwiches and Snickers bars. It is quite another thing to use your catering skills to demand love with menaces. And sadly, some mothers do. A missed dinner, or a dish not finished with great gusto is taken as a personal slight. Meals become a test of love and obedience and gratitude. And then they can become a breeding ground for starving and bingeing.

Sometimes a girl will decide to follow a daft diet because she wants to lose a little weight, or to keep her best friend company, but it isn't likely to run out of control unless she has something else on her mind. Like not wanting to grow up. Shrinking down to five and a half stone and putting your ovaries out of action is a very effective way of staying juvenile.

Prevention is always better than cure. A girl's best chance is to grow up in a family where food is enjoyed but not worshipped, with parents who give her the opportunity to grow up, but also allow her room to play up and to regress if she needs to. It is inconvenient that fifteen-year-olds want to be treated like adults one minute, and thumb-sucking babies the next, and parents never know which mode they're in until they've spoken to them in the wrong tone of voice, but it's a fact of life. It will also help if she has a mother who seems happy in her own skin, and if there is a minimum of preening and comparing of waist measurements.

An innocent remark from Uncle Stan – 'My word, you're getting a big girl. I can remember when you used to sit on my shoulders and sing "This is the Way the Lady Rides". I think I've got a photo somewhere' – can be all it takes to start a girl hating her new shape. And the idea of a disease that will enable you to wear a size 8 can be surprisingly attractive. My own teenage daughters were mesmerised by the experience of a friend whose weight loss was so drastic she was admitted to hospital. She was the talk of the gang. And I sensed that they were as excited by her setbacks as they were by her progress. They were impressively well informed about the risks to her future health, they visited her, enquired about her often, and treated her with affectionate concern whenever she came out for a day. But mainly, I'm sure, they looked at her hollow cheeks and skinny legs, and thought it would be quite nice to look like that themselves.

Some teenagers are never attracted to the idea of replacing meals with drinks that stick to your innards and make you feel full. They prefer the Real Thing, as served by Burger King, Colonel Saunders, and that hot dog man who fries his onions in dirty oil. Worrying about what your child *is* eating is a lot less painful than worrying about what she *isn't* eating, but it does still hurt. How can anyone choose a Double Gristleburger with Chilli when they could be home eating your fish pie?

The consolation is that a growing teenager may be able to manage the fish pie *and* the burger, all in the same evening. At times his appetite will seem insatiable, and as he spends less time at home so you'll lose much of your influence over what he eats. At home you may re-stock the fruit bowl every day and refuse to buy sacks of popcorn, but the moment he steps outside your door with a little money to jingle in his pocket, he will have access to the kind of food he really loves – plenty of salt, lashings of fat, buckets of sugar – and all wrapped up so he can eat it on the hoof.

You have no control over what your teenager eats away from home. And the sooner he learns to make his own decisions about health the better. But I think there is a strong case for sticking to your guns at home. However much he may gripe because you hardly ever give him chips, he'll still eat what you give him, because he's hungry. And every time he eats proper food, instead of hanging round the bus station with a bag of Hula Hoops, you score a quiet nutritional victory.

Eating rubbish can take years to catch up with you, and a fifteen-year-old has no means of imagining what it would be like to be forty-five, with angina and a full set of dentures. In my family the words Nice Crunchy Apple have become shorthand for the cruelty I've shown my children. I'm unrepentant. Away from my table I know they are awash with cola and fries, and yes, they do look perfectly healthy. But they're young. Their bodies have a lot of hard living to do. I tell them 'No we're not getting a soda stream. Nor a microwave. Shut up and eat your cabbage. I want you around to look after me when I'm eighty, not six foot under with clogged arteries.'

It would be useful if you could put your hand on your heart and tell your teenager that chips and chocolate mean spots, and salads don't. But you can't. Spots are essentially due to the effects of sex hormones – which is why it is possible to have greying hair, an exemplary diet and an erupting chin. None of this is of any interest to the teenager who looks in the mirror and sees nothing but lumps and bumps and craters, and a ruined life. What can you do to help?

Sadly, words of tender loving kindness do not act as a salve. When you are fourteen and you appear to be growing a second nose it follows that the attention of the world will be focused upon it. On the school bus, behind the bike sheds, in plenary session of the European Parliament, there will be talk of little else. So to have your Mum saying 'Spot? I can't see a spot. And anyway, you've got a lovely smile' isn't comforting. It's downright irritating.

So the first thing you can do to help is stop pretending. Then you can be a source of useful practical information. There are plenty of people who believe you can get spots if you look at a bar of chocolate, or if you think lascivious thoughts about Janice who works at the newsagent's. There are people who are convinced you'll get spots if you don't scrub with disinfectant three times a day, or if you sit next to Zitty McLachlan in Geography. As an informed and sensible adult you can set their minds at rest.

The only dietary step that seems to make much difference is to drink more water. The only skin care programme worth following is a gentle one. And there is no such thing as an overnight remedy. This is very hard to take when you've just arranged a date with a goddess from the Lower Sixth and something the size of the Matterhorn has started peeping over the top of your collar.

Spots have a natural life cycle. You can't strangle them at birth. Instead of dashing out to buy yet another miracle cure, time and money will always be better employed on camouflage and distraction – a jumper with a higher neck; a little carefully applied concealer; a self-confidence implant. A teenager who intends going out for the evening wearing a balaclava helmet back to front will take some persuading that personality counts, but it's always worth the try.

Strangely, the teenager who spends hours scouring and disinfecting his face often neglects the rest of his body. He checks hourly for new blackheads, and charts the most minute changes in his loathed and troublesome complexion, but with his acrid armpits and his rancid feet he is completely at peace. Frankly, he needs telling.

This is an almost exclusively male problem. Teenage girls become aware of the importance of personal hygiene when their periods start. In fact, 'Will people be able to tell because they can smell it?' is one of the questions girls often ask. Boys don't think about how they smell until they want to snuggle up next to a girl, and not always then. But someone has to point out to them that the hairy armpit of a fifteen-year-old is not the same thing as that pink little place you used to tickle with baby power. And no one loves a lad who never cleans under his foreskin. There's no point in hinting. Buying him a nice new sponge-bag won't work. If you don't tell him someone else will, so you may as well save him the mortification.

You're his parents. You can't expect to win popularity contests.

The physical changes in a teenager are so profound and so emotionally weighted it's a wonder teenagers don't all go into a neurotic collapse. Most of them weather the storm very well, and keep their darkest fears and what they think may be their daftest questions strictly to themselves.

Why am I the only fourteen-year-old girl in the universe who hasn't had a period? I'm definitely a boy, so why am I growing breasts? Can a tampon get lost for ever? Why did I get an erection in Trigonometry? If I shave my legs, will it grow back like Guy the Gorilla? Why is one breast bigger than the other? Why is Cunningham-Lambert's willie longer than mine? And which of us is normal?

Teenage girls generally find it easier to get answers about the things that worry them most. Because the start of menstruation is such a landmark in her life, and because her first period transforms her into a special consumer, a girl gets inundated with pamphlets and free samples and little talks from Nurse. In the name of enlightenment some co-ed schools now let the boys listen as well. But what boys really want are booklets that celebrate their first ejaculation. They want to know about dry runs and wet dreams and lumpy semen. They want to know everything there is to know on the subject of stiffies, and if they could have it all in a handy book, that they can keep in their room and refer to without anyone seeing which pages are the most thumbed, then so much the better.

Some parents get cheap laughs out of the cataclysm of teenage development. Couch potatoes with fallen arches, who have nothing to teach anyone about the Body Beautiful, think it perfectly acceptable to make a joke out of the fluff growing on their son's top lip. Friends they bump into in the supermarket are told that Alison just got her first bra. When Simon's voice breaks it is reported in the annual letter to Perth, Western Australia. And people who would die if they heard anyone talking about *their* vital statistics, never miss a single opportunity to say 'Just look at those feet. It'll take a hurricane to blow you over. Audrey, have you seen the size of this lad's feet? And you know what they say about men with big feet? Now what's upset him? You can't say anything to him these days.'

Well actually, how long is it since your voice was sliding up and down three octaves and your feet looked too big? It can't be so long ago that you've completely forgotten how awkward you felt, how easily your feelings were wounded, how much you hated the tactless old fart in the cardigan and slippers who reported it to the BBC World Service the first time you used aftershave. So why don't you shut up?

4 *A Nice Sports Jacket*
Teenagers and fashion

It's a funny thing, that the generation that threw off collars and ties and corsetry and spent its own youth in miniskirts and dungarees, is now the generation that worries what its teenage children are planning to wear to Grandma and Grandad's Golden Wedding party. Tamed by years of office protocol, and dressing to appease bank managers and golf club secretaries, most of us have rolled over and slipped graciously into something tasteful and subdued. That's fine. Middle age, pragmatism and well-cut navy wool make very good bed-fellows. But some of us go a step further. We insist on saving our teenage children from wrecking their lives by the injudicious wearing of an Iron Maiden T shirt.

If you can't go round looking colourful, bizarre or challenging when you're a teenager, when can you? Probably not until you're old, and beyond needing to create a good impression. If you get browbeaten into a nice jumper and skirt when you're fifteen, you may have to wait until you get a pension book before you can wear anything brave. You may have to spend forty years dressing for the office, the school gate, and then the office again. As parents I think we should take vicarious pleasure in the liberties our children take with fashion. It has to be one of the most refreshing things about them, especially in these drab, conformist times.

Today, in the world of teenage image creation, there are two strong trends. One is the targeting of younger and younger children, often long before their teens, wth scaled-down adult fashion messages. The other is the broadening of ideas about what looks beautiful. The first is a sad and cynical bid to catch consumers young and get them hooked. The second must surely be a welcome sign of self-possession, curiosity and tolerance.

In the Fifties, either you had a lift-and-separate brassière and a home perm, or you were beyond the pale, eccentric, perhaps with artistic leanings. In the Sixties we made a revolution. We opted for comfort and practicality, and the torch we lit then has never gone out. Girls today do wear corsets, but they wear them so they can be seen and admired as conversation pieces, not because of the secret shame of midriff bulge. Mainly though, they choose clothes that allow them to bend and stretch, and shoes that they can run in. They have also taken every prissy little idea we ever had about what goes with what and trampled it under their Doc Marten boots.

There is something hearteningly confident about them, even if they do spend Saturday afternoons haunting the changing rooms at River Island. They dress up as readily as they dress down, and their talent for recycling is impressive. The more threadbare something is, the more history it has, the better they love it. My teenagers are all fully paid-up members of a massive clothes swapping club. Nothing goes to waste. Nothing is so ancient, tattered, or just plain hideous that someone can't use it for something. And there is a wonderful generosity of spirit that allows them to enjoy seeing someone else wearing their purple Lycra leggings.

The dark side of this joyful celebration of youth is that some people disapprove of it, and rush to form a very low opinion of anyone with three earrings or air-conditioned jeans. Teenagers have to realise what they may be putting on the line if they refuse to make any concessions towards people who have jobs or college places in their gift. It may be their first encounter with narrow-mindedness and humbug, but of course it won't be their last. As parents we have to persuade them that working the system is often the smartest thing to do, and that it is possible to make the right impression – whatever that happens to be – without dealing a death blow to your individuality. When you're sixteen, wearing something clean and well pressed for a half-hour interview can feel like a major sell-out.

Given a few hours' notice the jacket situation or a trouser crisis can usually be resolved. Most families have the resources to put together Something Smart, by borrowing, adapting, or running to a chain store ten minutes before closing time. I have found this to be a much more successful method than trying to ensure that at any given moment each of my teenagers has something fit to wear to a Buckingham Palace investiture. I know families that maintain their teenage children's stock of tweed jackets and Viyella frocks, in readiness for the occasional christening, wedding or visit to Dowager Auntie Phyllis, and dutifully replace them, often unworn, when they're outgrown. It seems like a shocking waste of money, and it doesn't necessarily achieve the desired effect. A surly face is a surly face even in a crisp new shirt and tie. And then, what do you do about the tattoo?

When we were young we used to threaten civilised values with our beehives and white lipstick, but it could all be washed away at the end of the day. Today's teenagers have much less regard for what they may want to look like tomorrow. Maybe they believe even less in tomorrow than we did, and we were the generation that hoped we died before we got old. We curled our hair, or ironed it to get rid of the curls, and if we were very daring we had our ears pierced. That was as far we went. Hair dyeing was something done by fast women who sat on bar stools. And the only people who had tattoos were uncles who'd been in the RAF and got drunk one night in Osnabrück. Teenagers now do all these things, and more.

The number of earrings worn is pregnant with symbolism. Two earrings, one in each earlobe, is timid and conventional. A single earring, much favoured by boys, may be a fashion statement, or a wind-up. It isn't particularly unusual to see young businessmen in suits wearing an earring. It has become acceptable in careers where sharp young go-getters and wheeler-dealers have made their mark. But not necessarily in the fourth form of Cleckheaton Comprehensive. Getting an earring can be a superb way for a teenage boy to annoy his father, break his mother's heart, and get sent home from school. Some parents see it as a smear on the family name. Some believe it raises questions about their son's sexuality, an earring having such girlie connotations. Personally, I'd be more concerned about the dangers of a boy's earring getting ripped off in a rugby scrum, and his earlobe with it. Multiple earrings, three, four, or even more – the length of your ear's rim is your limit – are an announcement of a serious intention to mutilate and adorn. The next step may be a nose stud or even body piercing.

Holes in the ears, holes in the nose, they all heal up and disappear if you stop using them. A pierced and studded teenager isn't barred for life from becoming a solicitor or joining the Chamber of Commerce. The only problem in the short term is that the holes are often home-made, or done without much attention to hygiene. An infected earlobe is bad. An infected nostril is worse. If those hazards can be avoided, by keeping the holes gently but thoroughly cleaned, and by not picking at them with grimy fingernails, the only pitfall to having a ring through your nose is all the jokes you have to weather from the cardigan and slippers brigade. Like a hairstyle, it doesn't have to be for ever.

A child's hair evokes all kinds of sentimentality. Little baby locks are kept and treasured, and Auntie Vi is still telling everyone what lovely curls you used to have when you're reduced to three strands and a shiny dome. When teenagers do dramatic things with their hair it can be more painful than any other physical evidence of their growing up. The unexpected sight of my daughter's shaven head made me feel sick and shaken. I associated a naked head with illness, or with imprisonment and degradation. It took me a few days to calm down, relax, and notice what an exquisite shape her head turned out to be. By then the hair was already growing back, and I was able to enjoy the thin, velvety covering, and the delightful confidence of a girl who'd realised she could be beautiful without all kinds of props and crutches.

Around about the same time, my teenage son grew his hair long and wore it in a pony-tail. His schooling suffered, because of the amount of time and energy he spent on a losing battle for the same rights to a pony-tail as the girls in his school. His cricket suffered too. Not because the hairstyle had shifted his centre of gravity, but because frankly he didn't get selected as readily as when he'd had a more manly cut. In the fullness of time he did change his hair. He also changed cricket clubs.

Unlike a pony-tail, a tattoo is for keeps. At least, removing one is so difficult that it should be assumed to be permanent. In spite of that it is becoming a popular and glamorous symbol of rebellion, especially among teenage girls. Magazines now run photo features on what famous beauties have had tattooed, and where. The very idea strikes horror in the hearts of parents, who know that by the time you're thirty you don't want to be reminded of anything about your teens, least of all that you loved someone called Gary, or you thought a small butterfly would make you look interesting, feminine and tantalisingly tough. You can buy stick-on wash-off tattoos in shops that sell stage make-up. Get some for any teenager who has ever looked admiringly at photographs of tattooed celebrities.

Dressing to provoke is hardly ever a teenager's intent. They just wear what they like, and are often baffled by the reaction they get. A teenager who goes to interview some local dignitary for the school magazine and wears a jersey that is slowly unravelling does not intend disrespect, any more than he does if he turns up at a memorial service in trainers. His ideas about disrespectful behaviour are sketchy, and anyway, his attitude is likely to be that no one truly worthy of respect will be that interested in the way people dress. Usually all you need to do is engage his imagination, and enlarge his understanding of the trivial things that can preoccupy quite sensible, decent people. That way you appeal to his sense of humour *and* get him into a pair of well-polished shoes, all in one go.

In other guises, provocative dressing can't be handled so lightly. When a teenage girl dresses for her own pleasure and satisfaction, she has to be asked to consider what else she may be signalling. With boys of her own age her sexual availability will be judged by her behaviour rather than by her clothes. Teenage boys take it absolutely for granted that girls wear clothes that are short and clinging. Girls don't do it to seduce. They don't have to. The boys are in a permanent state of arousal anyway. The danger is from older, more predatory men.

Girls need to understand how prevalent the idea still is that men are helpless, explosive sex machines, never fully in command of their own bodies. Claims of contributory negligence evoke a lot of sympathy, and not just amongst men. Whether you see men as hormone-driven beasts or as humans with the capacity to understand 'You may look but you may not touch', parents should do all they can to mobilise a daughter's instincts for self-preservation. Her body may still be quite childlike, and her own enjoyment of it, dancing and laughing and generally messing around, may be naive and innocent. Unfortunately that may be exactly what men find exciting. If a girl insists on dressing as she pleases, the best precaution she can take is to do it in a crowd – a minimum of four friends, and preferably many more. If he can't isolate her, a predator can't do any more than look.

There are styles of dress that immediately define teenagers as targets for trouble from other teenage tribes. Flocks of black, flapping Goths; herds of baggy, saggy Ravers. Instead of safety in numbers, there is a real danger of pitched battles. But the problem is as old as time. The Woad Warriors probably used to slog it out with the Wolf Skinnies, and when their parents warned them to tone it down a bit they probably looked truculent and put on another coat of war-paint.

There is a period during the teens when to belong is more important than anything else in the world. Saying you belong is one thing. Wearing the uniform makes it real. Parents who hurry to catch the 7.43 every morning in grey suits shouldn't find that so difficult to understand.

5 *The Price of Peace*
Teenagers and money

Money is the key to so much independence. The question is, how much? And where should it come from? A seven-year-old can finance his taste for comics and sweets out of his pocket money, and use money he's given for his birthday and Christmas to pay for anything bigger. And there's always the possibility of topping up any shortfall by doing jobs around the house and getting paid for them. Teenagers live in a different world.

A teenager has a social life to maintain, an image to culti-
vate, hobbies to pursue, and eventually, a love life to invest
in. A ticket for the cinema or a gig costs a fiver. Audio
cassettes, videotapes, and styling mousse are considered essen-
tials, not luxuries. And £90 is the going price for a pair of
trainers with the right label. However much we denounce it
and declare that it's nothing to do with us, someone has to
take responsibility for whipping these young people up into
such a fervour of consumerism. However much we may snort
and disapprove, that is their world, and we helped create it.
When a teenager is forced to live on the margins of that world
because he just doesn't have that kind of money, he has big
problems.

The dangers are obvious. The pressure is on teenagers to
line their pockets, honestly or dishonestly. From the age of
fourteen my own children got jobs, starting with paper rounds
and then moving on to part-time work, evenings or weekends,
clearing tables, washing dishes, sticking labels on mail-shots.
That was one way round it. Other teenagers I've known have
preferred to join the Stolen Car Stereo Exchange Rate Mech-
anism, or the Dead Easy Money Option, selling spliffs of
dope. I can understand why. Their ways of making money are
perceived as much more glamorous than sweeping up hair in
a barber's shop. To hear them talk you'd think they were
Robin Hood.

I've also seen a few teenagers locked into a pocket money
arrangement because their parents are so fiercely opposed to
children working when they could be studying. Some just
break out, driven by the spirit of private enterprise. The more
acquiescent ones put up with having money drip-fed to them,
and only when they've satisfied their parents that it's for an
absolutely essential item. I feel sorry for them. There can be

few things more humiliating than having to justify £5 for a black hessian schoolbag when you already have a perfectly lovely leather briefcase that makes you look like a divvy middle-aged accountant.

A paper round can be a very reasonable, modest compromise. It gives a teenager a taste of routine and commitment, it introduces him to the world of work and gets him used to taking orders from irrational, befuddled adults who behave more like Mussolini than newsagents, and it provides him with the gratifying chink of money in his pocket. The only problem is safety.

These days some of us live near streets and high-rises where crimes of violence are common, and help is never near to hand. Add a dark wintry morning, and being a paper boy or girl can become a hazardous occupation. My children, whose greatest problem delivering morning papers in an inner city was getting up in time to do it, were supposed to carry a referee's whistle with them and blow it loudly if danger loomed. The idea was to deter an attack by making a fuss, rather than to try to raise the alarm – a very difficult thing to do nowadays, even if you scream and shout 'Murder!' Quite often they forgot to take the whistle with them anyway. But another family I know of dealt with the safety problem in a much more inspired fashion. Their son did his paper round accompanied by their large, mean-looking dog. He went about unmolested, and the dog got an extra walk.

Earning money is one problem, handling it is another. There may be a branch of your bank conveniently nearby, but there's likely to be at least one record shop or hot dog stall she has to get past before she reaches the safety of Deposits & Withdrawals. And banks are so keen to woo teenagers before they become regular wage-earners that they readily offer them cashpoint cards. So even at seven on a Sunday evening it isn't that difficult to finance a flame-grilled whopper and a chocolate milk shake.

The teenager who has enough self-control to handle a cashpoint card is a rare bird. The bank won't allow him to get into debt, but it won't slam down the portcullis until he's emptied his account. At the very least a teenager needs a bit of guidance about putting some of his cash beyond the reach of impulsive spending. Then he should feel free to do whatever he likes with the rest. The whole point about personal spending is that it is personal. You would probably find it as hard to explain the allure of a bottle of Burgundy or a year's subscription to *Practical Householder* as your teenager would to explain why he would rather have a poster of Sherilyn Fenn and a bag full of Crunchie Bars than anything else in the world.

Teenagers are so notoriously desperate for money that they stop getting parcels on their birthdays and at Christmas. Instead they get crisp £10 notes which disappear into the maw of some High Street cash till the minute the shops reopen. I think that's a pity. To get *some* money is certainly a treat. To get *all* money reduces the celebration to a quick pay-off. We might just as well remember our loved ones and their special days by direct debit. I understand the convenience of sending a cheque to a nephew you never see, and who anyway will be delighted to get it, but I think parents and others close at hand should keep up the tradition of parcels, containing things you never dreamed of, and things that belong in someone's nightmare. A carefully chosen gift is one of those important creative ingredients, between the earning of money and the spending of it, that give it any meaning at all.

The other kind of financial arrangement that parents get

into with their teenage children is an allowance, and most commonly, a clothing allowance. This can sound rather grand. The sort of thing Bertie Wooster depended on. But it can be very modest. The sensible idea behind it is that the teenager is given some real responsibility for money management in an area that will excite her interest – her clothes. I tried it with two of my teenagers, from the age of fourteen for a trial period of one year. Once a week I handed over the Child Benefit I'd drawn on their behalf. In those days it would have been £5–£6 a week, which amounts to about £300 a year, and is more than my annual expenditure on clothes, but then, I'm not a growing, evolving party-going fashion freak. The clothing allowance had to cover everything except school uniform, and a basic stock of socks and underwear.

My daughter managed creditably. She bought her fair share of rip-offs, eyesores and unmitigated disasters. She quite often hadn't got a thing to wear. And then she discovered those well-trodden routes to a larger wardrobe – thrift shops, and home dressmaking. After a year she begged to go back to the system where every spring and autumn your Mum or Dad takes you out with a cheque book and does you proud.

My son tackled his clothing allowance in different style. He already had the good foundations of an Orphan of the Storm look: ragged trousers, shattered T shirts, moth-eaten jumpers. He decided to stick with that image for at least a year. At the end of that time he had bought no clothes, but his clothing allowance had all gone, spent on records, books, cans of hairspray, pizza and joss sticks. He begged for another year's trial. I refused and withdrew the allowance. But funnily enough, the first time I tried to take him out and buy him something new to wear, I met resistance. It turned out that he was not so much a bad manager as simply uninterested in clothes.

I've tried to keep my teenagers aware of what things cost, but it hasn't been easy. Telephone bills didn't interest them, but an itemised bill strengthened my hand when I put a limit on the number of calls they could expect to make without paying. I've made them shop with me at the supermarket. But I find they're more likely to say 'If I'm quick can I go and get another packet of biscuits?' or 'Why don't we ever have roast beef? Lisa has roast beef every Sunday' than they are to say 'Cor! You don't get much for £35.70 do you?' My pledge to pay for their driving lessons until they passed their test or we collided with Mars, whichever was the sooner, was gratefully received and then taken utterly for granted, with cheque after cheque being thrown at the Department of Transport and Trev's Academy of Rapid Results. When one of them started pricing third-party insurance for a very ancient Volkswagen Beetle, there was a noticeable sobering up and counting of small brown coins.

With money, as with just about everything else, self-interest is the most effective teacher.

6 Old Enough To Drop It, Old Enough To Pick It Up
Teenagers and housework

I know what I mean by housework. You know what you mean. It's all that stuff that has to be done to maintain a certain quality of home life, from anticipating and planning through to the sweat and toil of its actual execution. Everyone in a family is affected by what gets done and what doesn't, and yet there is hardly ever any discussion about what is essential, what is a luxury, and who should be responsible for what. At the heart of most modern households there stands a woman, overworked, under-aided, who dreams of a world in which other people notice when the lavatory needs cleaning.

The harsh reality is this – housework is the pits. It's relentless, unsatisfying and unrewarded, and no one in their right mind would do it if there was any way out of it. What separates mothers from the rest of humanity in this is a sense of duty. It is what drives women who have jobs outside the home, and calls on their time and energy as parents, friends, children and citizens. They sense that they and their poor weary bodies are all that stand between civilised family life and Severe Carpet Odour.

Wherever there is a woman there will also be the assumption that housework is her thing. She may rise to great professional heights. She may become Chairman of the Milk Marketing Board, or Attorney-General, but the only way she's ever going to side-step the question of whose turn it is to mop the kitchen floor is by paying someone a proper wage to do it. On her back she carries the burdensome tradition that it is often quicker to do a job yourself than to teach it to someone who doesn't want to learn.

Some mothers believe that if only they persevere, their teenage children's resistance to helping around the house will crumble away. They believe that the fourth or fifth time their son cleans the bathroom sink he's going to think 'Hey! This isn't so bad after all! In future I'll save Mum the bother of asking me and just go right ahead and do it.' They are doomed to a life of disappointment.

Perseverance has nothing to do with it. With teenagers, as with most men, each time you negotiate for some help with the housework you are starting from scratch. If your daughter vacuumed the stairs three weeks ago it's very unlikely she's expecting to have to do it again. For one thing, she may have blotted out the whole distasteful episode from her memory. For another, she may think cleaning the stairs is something you do once and then it lasts for life. Teenagers have to have housework explained to them, first of all in general – about the inequity of one person servicing the needs of able-bodied idlers – and then in particular, as in 'The waste-bin is over-flowing. Would you please empty it before you go out?' The trouble is, a lot of mothers behave as though their children are mind-readers.

You have to ask clearly for what you want. If you are the tiniest bit tentative it will be assumed that you're not actually all that bothered. Furthermore, it is advisable to add a time frame to your request. If you just ask for the waste-bin to be emptied your teenager may well think 'Waste-bins do need emptying from time to time. Mum works hard, Dad works hard. Why should they always have to do it? Yes, one of these days I'm going to show willing and empty that bin. I wonder what's on TV.' And if you have any special requirements, if there are any standards that must be adhered to if getting the job done is to be worth anything at all, then you must explain that too. No one is born knowing you don't boil wash a lamb's-wool jumper.

As a parent I have tried democratically run Family Councils, I have tried looking tired and tight-lipped, weeping, screaming and lying on the floor and holding my breath, and I have tried rotas. Rotas were the least successful.

Six-year-olds get excited about rotas. They especially love drawing them up with their coloured pens. They then adhere to the rota religiously for a week. And then they forget. Teenagers just forget. Or they wait until you've juggled it around and tried to be fair and reasonable to all concerned, and then present you with all kinds of extenuating circumstances that might release them from mowing the lawn on Saturday. The most efficient method is to establish that certain jobs are the joint responsibility of every member of the family, and then, when one of those jobs needs doing, tell someone it's their turn.

Jobs of a strictly personal nature shouldn't feature in battles over housework. Any child over the age of five can put out his dirty laundry, put away his clean laundry, make his bed, and clear away his dishes. And he should. A teenager who's been changing his own sheets for ten years won't suddenly expect his mother to do it for him. He may step down his sheet-changing sessions to three times a year, but that's another matter. The areas of joint responsibility are something different.

Circumstances change, and so do work loads. To make each teenager individually responsible for washing and ironing his clothes easily leads to traffic jams at the ironing board, and queues forming next to the washing machine. But if every teenager is shown how to clean a room, sort and load a machine wash, and cook a few simple meals, you then have a crack auxiliary team at your disposal. You can say 'I need a night off. Nicky, please make sure everyone has a clean shirt for tomorrow. Daniel, corned beef hash for three please, as soon as you like', and be reasonably confident of getting what you want.

Reasonably confident. Teenagers hardly ever refuse point blank to do a job. They are more likely to make placatory noises and then disappear, or, if they are clever tacticians, to make such a dog's breakfast of a job that they think they will never be asked to do it again. This is why it's so important to be specific about how soon you need a job to be done, and to show them, the very first time if possible, how to do it. Laying down guidelines always sounds friendlier and more positive than finding fault after the event.

If a teenager says she'll do something and then doesn't, don't jump to paranoid conclusions that she's trying to drive you into an early grave. There is often some simple, innocent reason why she didn't wash the dishes. She may have thought you meant 'Wash the dishes when there is no longer a clean spoon in the house.'

Asking for help in a straightforward unapologetic way is a revolutionary thing to do for those of us who had stoic mothers. Many of us grew up in households where women stayed on duty beside the dolly tub and the mangle well into the second stage of labour, and where the wiping of a few plates by a husband or a child was cause for abject gratitude. We have to get accustomed to the idea that our teenagers are competent, able-bodied people, with an understanding of concepts like fairness and teamwork. If they leave undone something they ought to have done, we have to tell them. And then, when they do it, we should say thank you, just like we would to anyone else for a job well done. Half the trouble with teenagers and housework is that their interpretation of words like *sticky* and *floorcloth* and *immediately* is not the same as ours. The other half is that we don't really believe they can learn.

7 2.4 *Children, and Other Myths*
The teenager and his family

When we think about home life in the Nineties our imagination is haunted by two mythological families: the nuclear
family – isolated, highly mobile and over-stressed, with 2.4
children, a father with an ulcer, and a mother on Valium; and
the extended family – secure, deeply rooted, and eternally,
infernally supportive, with Auntie Phyllis in the kitchen
making dumplings, and Grandad nodding off under an apple

tree. For better or worse, most of us do not live like that any more.

The majority of households with teenage children are now single-parent families, or re-mixes of previously shattered families. This means that they have many of the problems of the nuclear family we all thought we belonged to, and the extended family we thought it might be nice to belong to, and then some. Money problems, unresolved losses, divided loyalties, and insidious pressures on those who are present to fill the shoes of those who are not.

Whatever the make-up of a family the basic position between parent and child is this – the parent wants the child to Do Well, and the child wants the parent to Ease Off. It isn't at all unusual for the child's position to be the more realistic of the two. Parents notoriously want their children to shine and sparkle in a way that they never could, to be healthier, wealthier and happier, and never to besmirch the family name. That's all.

When a parent is absent, or is a recently arrived interloper, the tension created by these expectations is sure to get raised a few notches. Where one parent is living away from the family because of a divorce, he may demand even greater proof that he has at least managed to sire some brilliant world-beating children, or, in the grief of dispossession, he may lose interest in them altogether. In either event, the pressure is on the children to stun and amaze, or to win back some attention by fair means or foul. With a step-parent on the scene, no matter how decent, loving and well-meaning they may be, the pressure escalates. A step-parent who has never been a parent before has everything to prove. A step-parent who already has children of his own is pulled in two directions. He wants his stepchildren to do well because a little reflected glory may oil the wheels of the new partnership, but he doesn't want them doing better than his biological children.

With fathers and teenage children the commonest problem is heavy-handedness. Sons have a need to test out as many aspects of their developing virility as possible, and Dad is an obvious target. Some sons need to wrestle with their fathers. Some need to battle verbally. Either need presumes that Dad is fit for the contest. But a lot of middle-aged Dads aren't. They are in crisis over their flagging careers and their decaying bodies. The last thing they want is to be challenged by some strapping young smart alec, and a common reaction is to lash out, like a bad-tempered old lion clouting a cheeky cub. He may flatten the lad permanently, or he may incite him to more daring acts of rebellion. Neither is very satisfactory.

Fathers and daughters have to negotiate the Little Princess problem. When the flirtation and manipulation that was once reserved entirely for Daddy starts to be directed at loathsome oiks with bulging crotches and no prospects, it is difficult for a father to relax. But what a teenage girl principally needs from her father is approval. Her self-confidence is fragile. Whether she has fulfilled the dreams her father had for her or not, she needs confirmation that she's bright *enough* and pretty *enough*. And, that whichever greasy-haired work-shy waster she chooses as her partner, Dad's back will be broad enough to bear it.

Mothers don't usually play the implacable tyrant. Mothers specialise in oblique manipulation. With a son, once he's grown bigger and stronger than his mother, psychology is her best weapon. An open, robust relationship between a mother and a teenage son can be enormously valuable to him as he forms his ideas about women. It can be the difference between him seeing women as people or women as doormats. But there is a danger. If the role of Father isn't being adequately filled, because he's not around, or because Mum makes it clear he might as well not be, a teenage boy can be quick to jump into the vacant position and play the big man. Once he's done that he can find it very hard to move on and star as the big man in the story of his own life. And his mother may not give him the encouragement he needs, because things suit her just the way they are. Thus are Mothers' Boys created.

Mothers and daughters have to go through the peculiar experience of growing apart whilst growing more and more similar. Mothers inevitably carry out the greater share of parenting. Little boys recognise from an early age that however much they love Mum they are destined to go away from her and become something very different. Little girls know that they will grow up, and maybe away, that they may achieve all kinds of things that were impossible for their mother. But they also know that they have the potential to become exactly like her. When a Mum looks at her daughter, she sees a past she may regret, and a future she can never really inhabit. When the daughter looks at Mum she sees an appointment with destiny, long before she's ready to accept it. That's what most of the screaming, stamping and breaking of hearts is about.

And then there are brothers and sisters, who know better than anyone else where to put the boot in. Some of the fighting that goes on between teenage siblings is no more than a sophisticated version of the old game of 'Tis! 'Tisn't! Physical jostling and sadistic wind-ups are considered legal currency by most teenagers, and the repercussions – the noise, the tears, the blood – bother parents more than they bother the children. But there can be more serious difficulties.

A younger brother or sister, who has yet to experience the

agonies of puberty, can embarrass or wound a sensitive teenager in magnificent style, especially in front of special guests. Little squirts who make loud announcements about Tracey being in love with her Maths teacher or Stephen growing pubic hair, need zippers fitting to their mouths. A child who is old enough to broadcast personal details is old enough to understand about respecting privacy. Whatever it takes.

And sometimes a teenager, feeling in need of more attention than he's getting, plays up at everyone else's expense. Parents who are embattled with a really testing, troublesome teenager easily overlook the toll it may be taking of their other children. I have personally witnessed brothers and sisters sleepless with worry over one of their siblings. And from the same source I've heard some very sensible, imaginative suggestions about what might be done. Such as 'Throw her out. But not until after Christmas.' When you are at your wits' end with one of your children, you can lose touch with what is sane and reasonable. A few words from the rest of your family, who have a grandstand view of what is going on, will help to set you back on the right track.

If you hear someone talking about a problem family you are likely to imagine a collection of tearaway children, who are always missing school and breaking the law and getting pregnant. Actually some very nice teenagers come from problem families. They have to cope with divorce, unemployment, abuse, gender battles, identity crises and the lack of any credible figure of authority, *and* acquire qualifications, a clear skin and a love life. They do well to come through the experience without completely breaking down.

The divorcing of parents is an enormous upheaval for teenage children, but not necessarily as damaging as we imagine it will be. In fact, the separation or the divorce may bring sad but rather welcome relief. The preceding fighting and the possible re-match that follows may be much harder to deal with, not least because parents often pretend their children know nothing of what is going on.

Some parents try very hard not to fight in front of their children. Instead they do it behind closed doors and with clenched teeth. This fuels the children's worries. Although it is frightening to see parents shouting and throwing saucepans, it is even more frightening to know that they are dismantling your life in silence. Children basically prefer their parents to stay together, even parents who should carry a government health warning. If staying together is out of the question their next preference is to be kept informed – not about what a repellent double-dealing piece of low-life their Mum or Dad has turned out to be, but about where the fighting leaves them. Usually they hope it leaves them loved and cherished by both parents, able to stay in contact with the parent who may be going away, and safe from any other major changes, like having to go to a different school.

Hope springs eternal, and teenagers certainly do their bit in the name of reconciliation. Playing up is their favourite technique. It is based on the premiss that if you present your estranged parents with a problem too big for either one of them to handle alone, they will be forced to work together, and that if they share enough dinners whilst trying to sort out a delinquent child, then romance may bloom again. Sadly, it hardly ever works. And neither does playing off one parent against the other, bouncing backwards and forwards with stories about meanness and generosity, kindness and cruelty, and non-stop partying versus the life of a Trappist monk. When teenagers resort to tale-telling and embroidering of the facts it is a measure of how desperately they long for their original family to be happy and whole again. And when one of their parents takes a new partner those hopes are dashed for ever.

Step-parents who take on teenagers are up against it. For one thing, the absent parent may be occupying a silk-draped marble pedestal. It isn't unusual for teenagers to vote with their feet as soon as they reach the age of sixteen and choose to move away from the parent who has had care, control and custody and move in with the parent who's taken them to the skating rink once a fortnight. The imminent arrival of a step-parent can speed up the process of deifying the absent parent and making plans to move in with him at the earliest possible date. This can be both a snub and a reprieve for the anxious step-parent. But for the parent who's had all the work for years it can be a crushing blow, and for the parent who's grown used to being adored from a distance it can be, er . . . not very convenient.

Single-parent families with teenage children settle into routines and patterns that suit them all. If the parent is strong and clearly defined as head of the household, it often works very well, especially without the conflict between two parents who differ fundamentally in their ideas about discipline. When everything is jogging along peaceably the last thing a teenager wants is some hot-shot lover moving in, with his Wagner CDs and his theories on the dangers of tight jeans and the benefits of National Service. Furthermore, a lover moving in can mean only one thing – a parent with an active sex life. For teenagers this can be a bewildering, ridiculous, and frankly disgusting idea.

The perception shift about middle-aged people and how they behave is real and recent. It isn't just wishful thinking by those now occupying the middle years. When we were children, middle age did have a negative image, for those living it and for those observing it from below. Fathers stagnated. They'd worked twenty years for the same company and only had another twenty to go before they could collect a gold watch. Mothers resigned themselves to an emptying nest and the ravages of the menopause. Parents did do things once their children were grown up, but it was mainly things like caravanning, and pottering in the greenhouse, and although they continued to have sex lives, it was mercifully invisible. Today's teenagers have to live with parents who are blatantly in the prime of their lives.

On the face of it today's middle-aged parents are healthier and faster on their feet. They've had the opportunity to taste more of life's rich variety, they have bigger hopes and schemes, and some of them have had facelifts. They are also less rooted. They are likely to have had to change careers at least once, moved house at least once, and changed partners. Today there is nothing unusual about a teenager having a mother who is a student, or a father who dates girls half his age and is about to lose his job. Nor is there anything unusual about having a Dad who's trying to find himself through hypnotherapy and the bottom of a bottle of Scotch, or a Mum who stays in her dressing gown all day and watches both showings of *Home and Away*.

Today's teenagers are presented with some very mixed messages. The old certainties about the roles of men and women have gone, and in their place there is confusion, and a background hum of anger. A family that has rejected the old ways and blazed a trail with alternatives – career *and* motherhood, fatherhood *and* career – does not always look very attractive. Sometimes, often, behind the pretty words there is an exhausted, disillusioned woman, and a baffled, offended man. A teenager may not examine the details of what's going on, but she will easily pick up that her clever, achieving Mum is as mad as hell, her politically correct, gentle nurturing Dad is ready to do murder, and still no one remembers to buy milk.

Parents often imagine that the zanier they are the better their teenagers will like it. They think their children will enjoy having a father who dresses like Elvis Presley. They are wrong. Teenagers are rather conservative, and they crave stability in their home lives. That way, if and when zany behaviour is called for, they themselves feel able to provide it. They would rather have a mother who cooks dinner than a distracted creature who's preparing paintings for her first exhibition. If she can manage both, all well and good. But. if she can't, dinner is favourite. Teenagers don't like parents who stay out all night, or who have friends round for chilli and beer, banging on about the future of the monarchy and flushing the lavatory till all hours.

They like parents who look nice, but not remarkable. Parents who seem as though they can look after themselves, parents who are *moderately* successful. They don't want you to have a procession of lovers bouncing in and out of your bed, making frank and fearless jokes about condoms. They don't want to read about you in the papers. And they definitely don't want to get home from school and find a note that says 'Gone to Jamaica. Chip money behind the clock.'

Of course, what they want and what they get may not mesh. One of the difficult tasks parents have to perform is gradually to move the focus of their lives away from their once-dependent children, back towards themselves. This may mean being unreliable, or even outrageous – both of them excellent things to be when you have older teenagers. This two-handed process, of letting go *and* keeping hold, may mean breaking the mould of perfect parenthood. And that should be a pleasure, not a hardship.

8 *The Best Days of Your Life*
Teenagers and school

There are many parents with teenage children who believe that when it comes to education a firm hands-on policy is called for. They want what is best for their children, and best is whatever they say it is. After all, they can remember their own schooldays as if they were yesterday, and they're not having their children make the mistakes they did. This can be a very dangerous attitude to strike.

Thirty years have passed since those parents were in school.

The world is a changed place. The reminiscences of someone who hung out in the Sixties may be of minor folkloric interest, but they have little relevance for teenagers faced with a shrinking job market, a wrecked environment, and shops full of crucial consumer goods they can't afford to be without but can't afford to buy.

The old routes that we could choose with confidence – school, university, apprenticeships, starting at the bottom, learning a trade, plodding slowly upward – are blighted now with potholes and blind alleys. Stupid people now do simple jobs with inflated titles, valuable scientists have to go to the United States to earn a living, and machines are mopping up jobs faster than anyone can create them. To tell your teenager that if she studies hard she'll be sure of a worthwhile job, a roof over her head, and society's good opinion, is to invite at least three different varieties of ridicule.

In the UK, education is compulsory for our children until they are sixteen. In fact there is less and less money and manpower available for chasing reluctant teenagers back into the classroom, so increasingly those who opt out stay out. On the other hand there is lot of pressure to keep anyone with the slightest inclination for education in school, and out of the unemployment statistics, for as long as possible. Many teenagers who are still in school beyond sixteen are there to stay warm, or to make good some of the gaps left after eleven years in full-time education – learning, for instance, how to write a formal letter or how to fill in a benefit application form.

Some children – please God let each family be blessed with at least one of them – some children know what they would like to do with their lives, and have the character and ability to make it start to happen. Then there are the children who want to become an overnight Hollywood sensation, or make a living collecting unusual pencil sharpeners. Eventually they may become civil servants or shop assistants or one of the other things no one ever plans to be. And then whatever rudiments of literature and arts and crafts and music they happen to have picked up in school may make an important difference to the quality of their adult lives. Parents who cling with white knuckles to the idea of their children getting to university at the very least, do well to consider this if evidence suggests they may have a potential filing clerk on their hands.

A parent's preoccupation with controlling what his teenager studies ceases to be healthy round about the time that big choices have to be made. Young teenagers need encouraging to try everything that's on offer. But older teenagers need to make their own decisions. This may mean letting go of your dreams of having a brain surgeon in the family. It may mean settling for a polytechnic instead of Balliol. But that's as it should be. You've had your turn at being brilliant. And if you made it clear, when your teenager was thirteen, that you were interested and concerned about her education, when she reaches sixteen she will understand that you are still there, that your advice and opinions are hers for the asking.

School can be many different things. For some teenagers it is purgatory. A lot of children are unhappy in school. A lot of parents think that is unremarkable and unimportant. I don't agree. Misery is certainly character-forming, but we already have a surplus of people who are vicious and unjust and determined that no one shall ever have an easier time of it than they did. Inevitably there is an element of tension in anyone's education, between the demands of self-control and conformity and the needs of the unique emerging individual. But by the time a pupil is in her teens she has had plenty of time to learn how to live in a large community and follow a few reasonable rules. By the time she's in her teens there should be more scope for her personality to flower, even if that means daring to tamper with the sanctity of a school uniform.

A parent I know, mortgaged to the eyeballs and beyond to keep his son at a first-division public school, explained to me that it was worth it for the standards that school would instil. 'Clean fingernails. Polished shoes. You know the sort of thing.' Indeed I did. But I thought he was buying some rather superficial standards at a very high price. Any fourteen-year-old who isn't brain dead will question the global impact of his not wearing regulation school trousers. As our children change from little people who need to do as they're told for their own safety, into big people who will be running the world the day after tomorrow, so we should expect and welcome the occasional challenge.

You can demand respect for your standards, but you won't necessarily get it. That's the trouble with demanding. Instead of respect you may inspire fear and loathing. A normal enterprising teenager will always find a way to work the system and beat the rules. But all that energy could have been used for something more satisfying. He might have been launching a new school magazine, or improving his French accent, or training for a charity run, instead of ducking and diving to get the better of Mr Swinley, the scourge of Trendy Hairstyles and Coloured Socks.

There are many ways to be unhappy at school, and most of them are endured in silence. Schools can be violent, frightening places. Teachers can be cruel. Other kids can seem to have power of life and death. And for a teenager who's struggling academically every class can seem like a pointless ordeal.

Parents who are only too willing to lay down the law about what subjects should be studied, how much homework should be done and which university should be aimed for often shrink from enquiring whether their children are happy, and if not, why not?

We should be more prepared to go into school and defend our children against things that are bigger than them. Bullying in the playground. Sarcasm in the classroom. Humiliation on the hockey pitch. For some reason, when they're faced with that kind of problem parents shy away, not wanting to be thought a nuisance. But pastoral problems aren't a nuisance to a really good school.

A nuisance is a parent who thinks his brilliant daughter should become a hairdresser. And a parent who knows his impenetrably thick son is going to make Queen's Counsel is a very big nuisance indeed. But a parent who makes a fuss about violence or intimidation, or even petty tyranny, is an asset to a school. No matter how intelligent a child may be, if he's frightened or browbeaten he won't perform.

Before you can address a problem you have to know it exists, and parents are often the last to realise. They may be so preoccupied with policing the amount of homework that gets done they fail to see that something is amiss. Truly conscientious parents are shocked when they get a call from school to tell them their child has been playing truant. And tummy aches that happen every Tuesday morning are dismissed as coincidental. School is central in a teenager's life. Its activities absorb most of her waking hours. It's where her friends are. If she suddenly doesn't want to be there, something is wrong. Finding out what isn't always easy.

My own limited catalogue, drawn from the experiences of friends and relations, lists only a few of the many things that can go wrong at school, and that a teenager may not feel able to talk about. Children handing over their dinner money to the playground mafia. Boys being gated because their hair is too short. Boys being gated because their hair is too long. A child becoming the butt of a teacher's sneers and taunts or sexual advances. Getting punished for someone else's crimes. Being paralysed with fear at the thought of having to sing, or recite, or run along a narrow beam in gym. Not being able to see properly, or hear. Becoming isolated because of one of those human conditions that brings out the very worst in others – being fat, or black, or having a stammer, or getting free dinners, or just being plain unapologetically brainy.

The argument about single-sex schools is set to run and run. The benefits and shortcomings are different for girls and boys. Teenage boys do many idiotic things, but they do not feign gormlessness in order to pull girls. An inability to do maths is not considered sexy in a boy. Nor is twittering and fluffing around in the science lab. But in a girl it may be. Some girls, a lot of girls, believe that displays of braininess damage their sex appeal. In a girls' school they are relieved of this worry. They can reach for the stars without prejudicing their chances of love. This is a powerful argument in favour of single-sex schools for girls, especially if a girl has social opportunities to meet boys and get a taste of their *otherness*. Any girl who has a brother gets a daily dose of that over breakfast and dinner anyway.

For boys in a boys' school the gains are less obvious than the deficiencies. Teenage boys will compete fiercely and argue strongly whether girls are around or not. But the presence of girls is influential in other ways. Girls tend to approach problem-solving with more flexible ideas, and they explain their ideas in a less adversarial style than boys. Their strengths, at drawing people out, and creating workable compromises, can transform a classroom discussion from thirty highly vocal ego trips into a truly educational experience. On the whole, the presence of girls has an improving effect upon boys. But the presence of boys can have a trivialising effect upon girls. If I could start again from scratch, I'd send my son to a co-ed, and my daughters to a convent on a small, remote island.

Whether or not there are the distractions of the opposite sex, the decision about how much to shine in the classroom is often a difficult one. This is hard for parents of today's teenagers to grasp. We grew up with an educational system that was constantly sorting people with tests and exams. 'You, go to the top of the class. You, over there to the Dunces' Corner.' We got tested, sifted and labelled, sometimes for life. Some children got despondent and gave up. But most kept trying. Coming top in History wasn't something you got embarrassed about in 1962.

The comprehensive system was bound to change that. In saving children from summary dismissal to the scrap heap it also put a brake on some of those who could have soared ahead. The pull of levelling has inevitably been downwards. And gradually, since the Sixties, playing down one's intellectual abilities has become the polite thing to do. British parents, when asked how their children are doing at school, will frame their answer in deprecatory style. 'Charlotte? Thick as two short planks. We're pinning our hopes on Textiles and Child-care.' We don't feel comfortable if we're discovered to have a foreign language, or the ability to add up our supermarket bill in our head. We put things down to good luck, or to being compared over-favourably with a room full of imbeciles. It has become chic to be thick.

This is reflected in more than standards of reading and

mathematics. It has also become a social embarrassment to talk clearly or write legibly. To betray any signs of having made an effort is to invite scorn. Teenagers, who have a desperate need to fit in and belong, are under enormous pressure to be dead ordinary. The ideal is to talk like a disc jockey from Basildon, and walk like a hustler from Brooklyn. To be caught in possession of a book or a sketch pad or an opinion is considered rather square. 'Dunno really' is the phrase that will take you absolutely anywhere. And really to excel at something, especially something that requires intellect, can be fatal to a teenager's street cred. This is how our teenage children are squeezed, between the hopes of their parents and the powerful downward thrust of their peers.

Is there anything parents can do? Plenty. Most of it amounts to just Being There. One of the first things secondary schools exhort parents to provide is a proper well-lit place to do homework. I don't know why. Anyone who has been five minutes in the company of teenagers knows that however much you spend on desks and chairs and adjustable lamps, the homework will still be done lying belly-down on the floor.

Items like year planners and desk organisers are quite unnecessary. Teenagers gather around them the accessories with which they feel most comfortable – mugs of cold tea, odd socks, apple cores, joss sticks, back copies of *New Musical Express*. Leave them for an hour, with Guns & Roses hissing on the stereo and an avalanche of jeans and T shirts threatening to engulf them, and they can produce a creditable essay on the Spanish Armada. Force them to sit up nice and straight and write with a fountain pen, and the creative juices may refuse to flow.

We learn things when we are ready, and good working habits are no exception. I learned to sit properly at my desk when neck ache finally got the better of me, and I devised my first filing system after I'd lost something very important. Unfortunately the lessons I've learned are of no interest to my teenage children. They want to learn their own lessons.

Homework is a thing you see very little sign of until there are difficulties. Then you are expected to have total recall of things you haven't studied for thirty years. Unless Naval Battles of World War I is your specialised subject, the best role for you to play when panic sets in over a piece of homework is to be the harbinger of calm and good organisation. It hardly ever matters that you don't know the answer to a question. It's far more useful to know how to set about finding it.

My own chaotic collection of books on a thousand obscure subjects was a standing family joke until my teenagers started doing homework and needed to know the chief world producer of cassava at nine o'clock on a Sunday night. Academic subjects are taught in much more exciting ways than when we were at school, and the material students are given to work with makes very good general reading. The problem is that often children don't know how to extract the information they need, or where to go if they want to know more. This is one way in which parents can be most helpful. Another is to play ignorant and try to provoke some good detective work.

A teenager who is in a hurry to finish his homework and go to the cinema is hoping for quick answers. You could probably take him straight to them. But you will do him a much greater service if you carry on knitting and say 'If you know what all those angles add up to, then you must nearly have cracked it. Write down what you already know, and then look again.' The satisfaction of working something out from first principles can be quite addictive, even for a teenager with sex and batting averages on his mind. Having a Mum who's got a PhD in gas crystallography isn't any help unless she uses her skills to get you to figure out things for yourself.

Exams were bad enough. Nowadays we have exams *and* course work deadlines. Assessment of course work is an excellent development in secondary education. It reflects a student's ability much better than just a now-or-never performance in the examination room. Syllabuses allow time for course work to be planned and considered, and this gives students the best possible chance to earn themselves a good grade. Unless they leave it all till the last minute, panic, botch it and threaten to run away to Argentina.

Teenagers have a poor sense of future. Tell them they have six weeks to prepare a file on The Development of New Towns, and they will think in terms of five and half weeks for reading *Viz* and trimming their split ends, and two days for panicking and camping out in the library. Those who plan ahead and work doggedly to a timetable are very few. Midnight oil will be burned. And you will be expected to provide coffee, sandwiches, glue, scissors and learned journals on urban planning. But really your job is to maintain a calm demeanour. You will probably want to say 'I told you not to cut it so fine. I told you not to go to that party. You've had weeks and weeks and all you've got is a street plan of Telford. Well don't come crying to me when you've children to feed and all the good jobs have gone to people who passed Geography.' Resist the temptation.

You may suspect that your teenager is dicing with her future, neglecting her school work. Seeing her report or meeting her teachers face to face may confirm your fears. What you do after that depends not least on your own self-assurance. The person who is messing up at school is your child, not you. You may have hoped for great achievements from her with bags of reflected glory for you, but realistically you stand or fall by your own achievements. Some parents doom themselves to a life of sustained disappointment.

Some children are simply not cut out for school. While others are getting merit marks, they are working out ways to escape. When they succeed they often do very well indeed. But while they are still reluctant students and you have to go to Parents' Evening and hear just how reluctant, it's hard to hold your head high. The golden rules are never to compare notes with other parents, and never to harp back – to how bright he was when he was three, or how his sister always got straight As, or any other irrelevant trip down memory lane.

Teenagers pretend to be indifferent to the expectations of their parents and their teachers, but they are painfully aware of them. Some parents don't want their children to get ideas above their station. Some parents won't be satisfied with anything less than their child being tipped for the Isaac Newton Chair in Very Very Advanced Mathematics. At sixteen, exam grades seem as vital to life as the beating of a heart. At eighteen, not winning a place to read economics, or getting a place and not taking it up, seems like the end of the world. Until you think back, to the class of '65. Where are they now? Did Carter make his million? Did Tunstall end up emptying dustbins? And did Bradshaw work out the meaning of Life, Electrons and All That?

And what about you? Can you remember what grade you got for Biology? Has Spanker Williamson's verdict that you were a waste of space and destined for a career assembling cardboard boxes been upheld? Aren't the things you now recall about school the friends and enemies, the injustices, the laughs, and the rare, truly inspiring teacher? And has there been anything that you skipped or flunked in school that you haven't been able to make good later if you really needed it?

The best subjects for *you* to study while your teenage children are in school are Objectivity and Philosophical Calm.

9 *The Oldest Hobby in the World*
Teenagers and sex

Sex is a problem. We all want our teenagers to grow towards full and fulfilling sexual relationships, but not where we can see it. And not yet. We want them to wait until they're married, or eighteen, or until they've finished their Duke of Edinburgh Gold. And when they do start we want it to be with someone clean and wholesome, and not in the back seat of a resprayed Chevette.

Our images of teenage sexuality are often wild and fantastic. One day your child is a fragrant innocent playing with his Fuzzy Felt. The next he is dribbling hormones all over the carpet. An unstoppable pleasure machine.

The truth is, teenagers have terrible sex lives. They have no expertise, and nowhere to go to acquire it. They fumble in bus shelters or do it very fast on the settee, listening for the sound of your key in the front door. No comfort, no privacy. And that's only the start of it. Love hurts. It makes you vulnerable and insecure. Sometimes it makes you so happy you lose all sense of judgement. But it is the kind of complication that goes with good sex. All teenagers understand this to a certain extent. This is why they don't actually do it on park benches, every night, with anyone they happen to meet who doesn't have three eyes.

The toughest thing to face about your teenager's sex life is that it's none of your business. It's one of the more private aspects of the grown-up self she's inventing. What you say, or think, or lay down on tablets of stone won't go unnoticed, but in the end may go unregarded. The parent voice is only one of many. And while you're wondering why your voice doesn't carry more clout, it's worth listening to some of the other incoming signals teenagers have to deal with.

In the UK the law says sixteen is old enough, but fourteen may be old enough for the confidential prescribing of contraception. Health educators point out that sex can now kill you. Sex manuals urge us to go for the multiple orgasm. Vice Sex Romps are served with Sunday breakfast. Auntie Pearl was relieved to stop doing it after she'd produced a son. Sexual abuse of children is internationally rife. Madonna gets paid a lot of money to play with herself on stage. Public figures risk everything for it. And the official line is that Jesus's Mum didn't do it at all.

The message is far from clear, but it runs something like – Sex can be one of life's pleasanter activities. Just watch out for the fear, shame and transmittable diseases.

Teenagers have sex lives. Only one in two is still a virgin by the age of eighteen. And it is an area of life which is almost entirely their own. Parents only become involved when the consequences of a teenager's sexual activity literally invade their lives – if your son has sex with an under-age girl in your house, you are involved; if your teenage daughter gets pregnant and looks to you to raise her child as though it were your own, you are involved; and if your teenager brings her partner home to make love behind her flimsy bedroom door in your well-appointed but non-soundproofed family house, you are involved, and so is anyone else who isn't stone deaf. Those situations apart, you are not involved. You can't control what they do or whom they do it with. Your role is to feel anxious and uncomfortable. If you don't, something is wrong.

There's another thing parents sometimes feel when they're confronted with a sexually active teenager. Envy. Don't bother. There is nothing enviable about the sex life of a teenager.

There are many places where ignorance is bliss, but bed is not one of them. And teenagers are sexual ignoramuses. Our hearts should go out to all those teachers who sweated bricks over sex education. They lost sleep trying to find the correct blend of chumminess and authority with which to discuss masturbation with 4C. They died a thousand deaths before they did the demonstration with a condom and a carrot, an *erect* carrot. All to very little effect. Teenagers still believe you can't get pregnant if you do it standing up, or if the girl doesn't have an orgasm, or if her period has just finished, or just started. Some of them still believe you can run out of semen if you do it too often, or that a five-minute bump and grind constitutes languorous sex. Don't envy them. Having your own teeth and buoyant breasts isn't everything.

The classroom is not the best place to relieve teenagers of much of their sexual ignorance, it seems. In spite of the noble efforts of teachers, the facts get remembered imperfectly, as novelty items with no relevance to the real life of a real teenager. Maybe there's just too much at stake. Before you can learn you have to admit, to yourself and your teacher, the things you don't know. And that could do untold harm to a teenager's public image of self-assured cool. If everyone in the gang thinks you've been screwing Big Beverley all summer, how can you admit that actually you've always wondered where you're supposed to put your legs? And especially to the balding middle-aged Year Tutor who knows the answers because *he's* done it?

A welcome exception to all that embarrassment and bluster has been the achievement of schools in teaching teenagers about HIV and AIDS. I find teenagers impressively well informed about these conditions, much more so than many of their parents. But in the next important step, translating the known medical facts into a personal code of safety, teenagers are not so different from the rest of us. They find it hard to believe that anything like that could really happen to them.

Humans don't take long to become immune to particular fears. Broadcasts that shock us the first time we see them soon become unremarkable. Rather than inundate our teenage children with warnings and horror stories, we'd do better encouraging them to read and watch critically and selectively. There is also increasing scope for teenagers to experience the impact of HIV and AIDS at close quarters by volunteering for one of the befriending schemes. A single instance of personal contact is worth a thousand pamphlets. In the end, something has to persuade our children that safe sex means protected sex, *every* time.

Not so long ago when a mother went through the pockets of the dirty laundry and found a packet of condoms it was the signal for hysterics. Never mind that it showed someone was taking responsibility for contraception. It was so blatant, so primitive. The neat little contraceptive pill had made the condom seem like something only horny lorry drivers carried.

But the increased incidence of sexually transmitted diseases has changed all that. Herpes, chlamydia and HIV have made condoms things we should be relieved to see when we're checking the laundry. I think there is a very strong case for condoms to be kept in every house where *anyone* has a sex life, or even the potential of one. Supermarkets sell them, so they can easily become part of the weekly routine – 'Do we need shampoo? Do we need toothpaste?' Just as long as they don't become the subject of an inquisition. 'Who used the last one? Come on! There was one here last night, and *I* haven't had it.'

One alternative to sex on the blackboard is sex in the comfy chair. That time-honoured, well-worn staple of family life, A Little Chat. The traditional Little Chat never worked. Mainly it came too late. A series of spontaneous mini-chatlets spread over the first ten years, dealing with questions as they arise, is much better. The Little Chat is usually a tense occasion, especially between man and boy. 'You may find you're starting to get . . . certain feelings. Nothing to worry about. All perfectly natural. When you get married everything will fall into place. The main thing is, not to dwell on it too much. Work hard. Enjoy your rugby. I'm always available if you have any questions. Oh and Mum asked me to give you this little packet. Remember son, don't die of ignorance.'

You can only learn about sex from someone if you feel comfortable asking them questions. This dramatically narrows the field of possible teachers, and excludes parents, who are handicapped on the following two counts: they are hopelessly out of touch with the sex lives of modern youth, which is obviously nothing like the stuff they were doing in 1965; *and* some of them are still hanging on, pretending to have sex lives of their own, which is a totally gross concept but thankfully is probably nothing more than obscene wishful thinking.

Teenagers learn mainly from each other. This was always the case, and for all its imperfections it is a method that works at least as well as classroom discussions. In the classroom some of the energy and attention that could be devoted to learning facts and discussing their implications gets drained away by confused bashfulness. In the Nineties we are all cajoled into being open about something that is essentially private. The really illuminating bits of sex are the personal bits. Not *how* to unroll a condom. A chimpanzee could work that out. But who does it, and at what point, and how each of you feels about it. That's the kind of thing you long to know when you're inexperienced, and you don't want to hear it from your Dad or your Biology teacher.

A parent's best hope of improving the quality of sex education their teenagers are passing around is to stock the house with good books on the subject, preferably illustrated, and the less solemn the better. Children will pick them up and look at them long before their teens. Friends who are being raised in book-free zones will fall upon them. In our house the covers had dropped off all of them years before we ever had a teenager.

Books are an excellent way of getting the facts straight.

Ethics are another matter. You may be able to find a book that deals with the very axe you wish to grind, but your teenagers are growing up in a world where there is no moral consensus on sexual behaviour. The best you can do is tell them clearly what you believe. You can add passion to clarity. Your children may eventually come to share your convictions, but maybe only in the light of personal experience. They may reject your views out of hand. Whatever the outcome, it is worth while putting down your own markers, in particular about what makes you uncomfortable. If you don't, your silence may be construed as laid-back indifference.

So in strolls your seventeen-year-old son with his sixteen-year-old girlfriend and asks if she can stay the night. Of course she can stay the night. Haven't you always made his little friends welcome? But he didn't mean that kind of staying the night. He meant in his bed.

He argues that he and his girlfriend already have a full sexual relationship. They do it anywhere they can find five minutes of peace and quiet, so why go through the pretence of bunking down chastely in separate rooms? The likeliest reason why is that you'll feel more comfortable. Feeble, but valid. If you disapprove of sexual relations outside of marriage, or between teenagers, or between your teenager and any other human being, your son will have to accommodate you. It may be his home, but you set its tone, and if you're not happy with what he's doing he may have to consider going elsewhere to do it.

If you name your criterion – marriage, for example – it's easy to get dragged into hair-splitting exercises. Would marriage really make the difference? Even if the bride was sixteen and the bridegroom seventeen? And what will be your position if your son forms a life partnership with someone without ever marrying? Instead of trying to find an answer to all of these reasonable questions, it is simpler and more honest to say 'Right now I'm not comfortable about you and your girlfriend sharing a bed in my house. If and when I am, you'll be the first to know. Until then, separate rooms.' Being a parent doesn't mean you can't be unfair or irrational some of the time.

Once you have accepted that your teenager will eventually have a sex life, whatever your opinions, you can address the areas of sexuality where you may have some influence: in particular, safety – physical and emotional.

At this point the gender difference becomes alarmingly important. Parents who've spent fifteen years trying to eradicate gender stereotypes from their Equal Opportunities nursery find this very difficult. Whatever our children experience and witness in their early years, whatever we do to encourage and develop feminine strengths in our sons and male strengths in our daughters, we end up with young men who feel driven To Do, and young women who expect to Be Done Unto.

My own feeling is that this shouldn't deter future parents from following the principles of sexual equality. I still believe the world will be safer in the hands of the emotionally well-rounded than in the hands of sexual chauvinists. But we have to be aware of the conflict we may be fuelling in those poor adolescent minds. We are asking our sons to be sensitive and tender, while their hormones are telling them to go for the explosive thirty-second screw. We are asking our daughters to be self-possessed, and to look beyond relationships for their achievements and satisfaction. Their hormones are telling them to find a big strong male and build a nest. How many of us, reared in the Forties and Fifties, were expected to resolve such enormous contradictions?

The level of sexual activity in a teenage boy is inversely

proportional to the amount of other activity in his life. So Baden-Powell was really on to something with the Scouting movement. Excitement and enthusiasm for school work, sports and other hobbies don't reduce the urgent need for sexual release, but they redirect it. Masturbation provides a very satisfactory alternative to complicated, time-consuming romances. It's quick, there are no risks, and you can hurry back to gluing your scale model of Ark Royal without having to tell anyone you love them.

So for a time, if you'd like to put a brake on your teenage son's sex life, you can help by encouraging him to do the other things that interest him, and, if you think there are any doubts in his mind, confirm once and for all that masturbation does not make you go mad, blind, hairy or hairless. No matter how often you do it.

When he makes the transition to sex with girls, safety is mainly a question of health education. This is not to say that young men are immune to passion and heartache. They can and do fall heavily. But the underlying importance of other things in their lives – career ambitions, the possibility of playing for the County team, the solace of messing around with a drum kit – these things see them through. The risk of a boy getting seriously messed up when a relationship fails or ends are much less than they are for a girl. The major risks for a boy are that he will become a teenage father, or that he'll catch a disease. Condoms will protect him against both.

The sex life of a teenage girl is complicated. She wants the experience of sex for its erotic content, and for the warmth and tenderness it may bring. She wants the emotional closeness of knowing another person intimately. She probably also wants to do well at school, keep up with her girl friends, read *Cosmopolitan*, and be looked after if anything goes wrong.

The chances are that unless she is unusually absorbed in some activity – playing an instrument, or training for a sport – by the age of fifteen, relationships will already have assumed prime importance in her life. Everything else she does is likely to reflect that. Her willingness to subordinate her own needs and wishes in order to nourish relationships with others makes her vulnerable. So does her fertility. Little wonder then if one of the messages a growing girl receives is that being a woman is dangerous.

This message used to be spelled out for a girl loud and clear. The messenger was her mother, or some other older initiated woman, and it was delivered through tightly pursed lips. 'Keep your legs crossed, young lady. Men only want one thing, and if they think they can get it for nothing, you're done for. And another thing. They may run after women who don't wear knickers, but they don't buy them three-piece suites.'

The thing that would do most to protect a girl from deep emotional involvement or pregnancy until she's really ready for them, is a well-developed sense of self-interest. And self-interest is the very thing she represses in her search for a mate. Teenage boys choose partners they find attractive and congenial. Teenage girls often choose walking disasters – rats and wimps and bigheads – whom they think they can turn into worthy members of the human race by lavish applications of devotion and love. A girl's future plans, in so far as they exist at all, involve finding a man and tagging along. It's hardly surprising that girls seem prepared to risk so much in the name of love. In their teens they have so few realistic ideas about the future that they can't possibly know what they're putting at risk.

Modern mothers, who've enjoyed the benefits of reliable contraception and more open relationships between the sexes, can unwittingly add to the confusion their teenage daughters feel. On the one hand there's Mum, still with a twinkle in her eye at the advanced age of forty-three, being up front and laid back on the subject of sex. And on the other, there are the old negative vibrations. A subtext about danger and fear. At the risk of appearing old-fashioned, this is what we should discuss with our daughters.

Never mind about where to find your G-spot. A girl needs to know that males and females speak different languages. A boy needs to know it as well, but he won't be as interested. Girls find it hard to accept how different a boy's investment in a relationship is from her own. He may make a genuine commitment to a girl, reveal himself to her, feel that he loves her, but at best the relationship will rank equal first with other important considerations, like work and play. A scenario in which someone else works and brings home enough for both of them has no place in a boy's fantasies about the future. He knows, in a way that a girl does not, even in the Nineties, that he will have to be a worker as well as a lover.

Girls are devastated when they discover that a boy can be in love but still love other things, and when they discover that boys easily uncouple love and sex. Men are not sex machines, but from the female perspective they can look that way. The difficulty a mother has is to convey to her teenage daughter how great the risks of love are, without paralysing her with fear. In this she's helped or hindered by her daughter's self-esteem. No matter what the subject, all roads lead back to this same delicate creature. If we spent less time worrying about oral contraceptives and provocative clothing, and more time encouraging our daughters' sense of self-worth, we would do very well indeed.

We assume that our teenage children will turn us grey haired with their heterosexual behaviour, and we hope, if only because of the difficulties they are bound to face, that we shan't have to deal with their homosexuality. But for some of us it will happen. And if the sex life of a heterosexual teenager is painful, that of a homosexual teenager is agony.

If he keeps his homosexuality secret then he has loneliness to endure as well all the other possibilities – self-doubt, shame, unrequited love. If he comes out he suffers a different kind of loneliness. In this, as in everything else, teenagers have a desperate need to belong, to have the approval of a crowd. Young homosexuals often feel as though they're in a self-declared Club of One. They are also aware that the first reaction of their parents will be negative. This may be outright homophobia, from the people who should love him unconditionally. It may be denial. Girls who announce their homosexuality are often told that no such thing exists, or that they are going through One of Those phases. Or it may be a kind of shell-shocked searching for something to blame – 'Where did we go wrong?' 'I always said we shouldn't have let him go to dance classes.' 'It wasn't the dance classes that did it. It was the way you went on and on about the rugby club not taking players with pointy toes.'

Scientific evidence that our sexuality is determined before we are born piles up relentlessly. But your next-door neighbours, and Grandma and Grandad, may not keep up with current neuroscience. They may just be of the opinion that you've raised a wrong 'un, and everything he ever did – writing poetry, wetting the bed, kicking a football through their kitchen window – and everything homosexuals ever did, will be laid at your door. Your homosexual son or daughter will anticipate all this and be tempted to spare you. If there is a single thing parents can do to help, it is to relieve their child's isolation. He needs encouraging to meet other gay teenagers in some sort of supportive setting. And if he does, you may get the opportunity to meet other parents. When you are dealing with Uncle Len, who believes all homosexuals should be put up against a wall and shot, these are the kind of friends for which you may be truly thankful.

Finally, an aspect of sex that is troublesome for teenagers but frequently overlooked – parents. Sexually active parents.

Teenagers have a skewed perception of senility. They think it starts at the age of twenty-seven. They also carry over from childhood some of their ideas about parents being more or less than human. Birds do it, fleas do it, but surely not the Old Folks?

Teenage children are probably most comfortable with parents who patently don't do it. When their parents are still obviously attracted to one another, or worse still when they are guilty of provocative behaviour, like going into the bedroom, closing the door and insisting that their children knock and wait for an invitation to enter, revulsion is a likely response. This is healthy. We have so few taboos left completely unchallenged these days, it's very comforting to see the question of sex between parents and children being dealt with at gut level. Some parents affect to be dismayed. 'We've told them,' they say, 'just because we've got a few wrinkles and Dad's losing his hair, doesn't mean we don't still enjoy a good bunk-up. And we shall still be doing it when we're seventy, thanks to KY Jelly.'

Pity the teenager with such merciless parents. It's enough to put you off it for life. Almost enough.

10 *Carefree Youth and Other Burdens*

Teenagers and stress

It may be hard to believe that your teenager, who rose at lunchtime, blitzed the kitchen and then spent the afternoon agonising over which shirt to wear, is a candidate for stress, but she is. Stress is an inseparable part of the modern human condition, so teenagers qualify. Some of the pressures on them are positive – the kind that get you off your backside and doing something – and some of the pressures are destructive. The problem for a teenager is not that the pressures exist, but that there are no safe and certain strategies for dealing with them.

Until recent times most teenagers lived within clearly drawn boundaries. Home was a place where Mum was always around, to service everyone's practical needs and provide a bosom to cry on. Dad went to work. What he did at work was the most notable thing about him, and he did it, for long, hard hours until he was sixty-five, and then he stayed home and got under Mum's feet. School was where you went until you could start out on your own little journey, through work and courtship, marriage, getting a place to live, becoming Mum and Dad, and repeating the whole well-tested cycle.

Now those boundaries are in a state of flux. Some have gone for ever. Some seem to be there, until you need to touch them, and then you find they've shifted. Teenagers cannot look forward to a life of honest toil even if they want to. The job market is shrinking and changing. Mum is no longer at home with the kettle on the hob, Dad is worried witless about redundancy, marriages are fragile, domestic violence is on the increase, and there's now nothing unusual about penniless, jobless teenagers setting up home in one small room and having babies.

And as if all that is not enough, we are subjected to the unremitting patter of people who want to sell us things we don't need and can't afford. Crime quite often does pay. And all kinds of activities that used to be safe, like having sex, or walking down the street, can now cost you your life. A teenager may not actually sit around with her head in her hands saying 'O woe is me. How can I make any sense of this mean and crazy world?' but her behaviour will betray her confusion and depression.

Teenagers are not supposed to get depressed. The very idea sets many parents off into gales of scornful laughter. 'Depressed! You've got no business feeling depressed. Arsenal are doing all right. And you've got that smashing twin-deck cassette player. I mean, take me. I've lost my No Claims Bonus, and the frost got my begonias, but I'm not depressed. Your Mum's got to have her veins done, and she's not depressed. So what have you got to be depressed about?' Quite often the most honest answer to that is, 'Nothing. I just am.'

It is a fact that teenagers are prone to depression – an invasive, debilitating black mood that doesn't necessarily relate to any particular problem in their lives. The teens are a time of struggle and change, as each unique adult identity takes shape. It is metamorphosis, without the privacy of a cocoon. It happens in full view of everyone, which makes it painful for the teenager, and uncomfortable for onlookers, however loving they may be. This can be bad enough. But if, for some reason, it doesn't happen, if the process is cut short, or never gets started, then something worse is in store – chronic depression, or some other form of mental breakdown.

A teenager whose parents have controlled her every child-hood move may never attempt the messy, exploratory phase of developing her identity. She may join something like an authoritarian cult and buy a ready-to-wear personality instead. Alternatively, she may settle for the identity her parents have foisted upon her, and sooner than offend or disappoint them, she'll succumb to the depression that goes with being an eternally perfect child.

Or she may short-circuit all that searching and wondering by pretending she's already done it. Teenagers who deliberately get pregnant or who marry are often using this strategy, faking maturity rather than slowly and painfully achieving it.

Sometimes the answer to 'What have you got to be depressed about?' is 'You.' The tradition that teenagers are awful encourages us to overlook the fact that many parents are absolutely appalling. They lie and cheat. They drink too much, or smoke. They pretend to know things when they don't. And they treat their children with contempt. You wouldn't want people like that as your friends, but if you're a teenager you're stuck with them as your parents.

Most of us, whatever our age, are resilient to depression. We experience it, but we bounce back. Having a job to do or other people to care for gives depressed adults exactly the kind of push they need, and if they need more help than that they usually know where to go for it. A depressed teenager is much more vulnerable. Exchanges with teenagers are based on the assumption that if you're sixteen years old and in good health you must also be feeling on top of the world. In the general course of conversation they're not given the space to unburden themselves, and parents, who should be better placed than anyone else to see when a child has problems, often have a very good reason for not noticing – *they* are one of the problems.

When a teenager wants to sleep all the time, or can't sleep at night, when she isolates herself from her friends, neglects herself, stops eating, or her school work takes a sharp downward dive, she is signalling that something is wrong. She needs to talk. An older brother or sister can be a good starting point, or an empathetic teacher. Grandparents can also make excellent one-step-removed listeners. Someone must do it. Teenage suicide attempts are on the increase, especially among boys, who tend to make a very thorough job of it.

When a teenager makes very vocal threats to harm herself, or highly visible attempts that are bound to be intercepted by whoever is looking on, it does at least mean that the lines of communication are still open. 'Look,' she is saying, 'I'm in such a mess I'm prepared to take risks with my own health and safety, and frighten everyone who loves me.' And sometimes, tagged on to this desperate message is an extra plea, 'Give me what I want, and I'll be fine.' Threats to run away, or open, ostentatious searching for pills on which to overdose are the kind of behaviour I have in mind here. Every example of this that I have ever seen has responded eventually to firmness combined with screaming, stamping, cuddles, bear-hugs, and a loving full Nelson on the sitting-room floor.

My own experience has been that quieter, stealthier attempts at self-harm should be taken very seriously indeed, even if they are unlikely to have fatal consequences. Any kind of really determined self-injury is an indicator that help is needed.

The first port of call, your family doctor, may be as far as you need to go, although after the age of sixteen your teenager is entitled to make her own decisions about medical treatment, and to full confidentiality with her doctor if she does agree to seek help. An alternative, depending on the nature of the problem, is to use one of the many counselling services that have mushroomed in the last ten years. Some are excellent. Some promise more than they can deliver. The trouble is finding out which is which. But word gets round. So ask. And for additional support with specific problems there is now an advice line for just about everything. I have included a list of these at the end of this book.

Parents who are neck deep in financial problems or matrimonial ones should not underestimate how abandoned and frightened their teenage children can feel.

When there is trouble at home, when parents are unhappy and constantly fighting, or when someone is seriously ill, the children, whatever their age, decide that some of it is their fault. They don't usually say as much. But inside they let it eat them up. A teenager who seems quite distant and independent from her parents can be devastated by the sight of her family disintegrating. It's commonplace for parents who throw knives or closet themselves away for hours for grim conferences to say, 'We haven't really involved the children.' It's yet another example of parents treating teenagers as though they're members of a different species.

In fact, they suffer the same grief and fear as everyone else but they get very little consideration. Unlike tiny children, who get treated with tender concern, and the adults who stand centre stage and become absorbed in the drama, teenagers are assumed to be more interested in getting on with their own lives. If asked, they will tell a very different story. They may see the family's problems with breathtaking clarity. And often they are beating themselves up because they think they may have made things worse. It is hard to believe that strapping sixteen-year-olds cry into their pillow because Dad's going away, or Mum looks haggard, or their sister has to have another operation, but they do. And it's hard to believe that a cuddle helps, but it does. Mostly though, they need to be told what's going on. They need to be included.

Sometimes the crisis involves the teenager and one of his parents. When that happens it's the other parent who feels as though they're on the outside looking in. It's most important that they don't stay outside. When a parent and child have locked horns, the other parent is involved, if only by default.

A common scenario involves Dad in the role of Relentless Ogre, Mum playing the Toothless Lioness, and a teenager cast as a Pawn and Punchbag. The main theme of this story is that Dad is constantly on the teenager's back, and Mum is constantly trying to drag him off it. Dad's weapon is usually a lacerating tongue. Dad never misses an opportunity to reduce his child, dignity and all, to the size of a garden gnome. Mum stands around wringing her hands and saying things like 'Give the lad a chance.' And the teenager suffers. He doesn't get proper protection, and he doesn't get reasonable limits set for him either. He just gets the message that whatever he does, Dad will disapprove, and if he's lucky Mum will kiss it better. A message like that is a curse for life.

When that sort of thing is happening it means there is a serious imbalance in the way the parents relate to their children. Ogres believe that if they don't knock people into shape, no one will, and then civilisation will collapse. They feel indispensable. They have to be forcibly relieved of some of their duties. The simplest way to achieve that is for the other parent to set limits and enforce them in a more visible way. A partner who recognises the imbalance and decides to shoulder more of the job of disciplining children gives the ogre an opportunity to back off. He may only back off a little; ogres find it very difficult to let go. But any respite you can give a teenager from endless nitpicking and nagging is a balm for his battered self-esteem.

Outside of family strife, the thing that most gets teenagers down is the future they may not have. For the very brightest, who are likely to take at least one degree, the question of what kind of work they'll end up doing is remote. But for the ones who would like to stop studying at the earliest opportunity, the problem is here and now. People who say the newspapers are full of job adverts don't always bother to read them. There are jobs, but they are mostly at the two extremes of the employment spectrum. There are jobs for those who have qualifications and experience. And there are part-time and casual jobs, for people who don't want or don't need any kind of life plan. In between there is very little.

For many teenagers the choice is to stay at school, unmotivated and frustrated, or to slide into a life of drawing benefit and making do. If you have a roof over your head and no responsibilities, a short stint living on benefit is not such a terrible experience. Kids who haven't got jobs hang around together and pool their resources. Some of them turn to private criminal enterprise. A teenager who sees her friends making a comfortable living out of shop-lifting or dealing in dope is going to be understandably tempted. On the whole, anything – sweeping floors, being a reluctant student, *anything* – is better than lying in bed waiting for the postman to bring your benefit cheque.

The search for work is deeply depressing. You can't get a job till you've got experience, and you only get experience by having a job. You can't even volunteer your able young body for service overseas any more. Those agencies only take people with special and useful skills. After weeks of nothing but rejection letters, it gets hard to climb out of bed every morning, let alone spend time trying to turn yourself into a more employable proposition. Things like learning to use a typewriter keyboard or getting a driving licence are sensible things to do. But when you're seventeen, and you want to be able to buy a leather jacket and a new CD every Friday but you can't even get a job clearing tables, you don't want to be sensible. You can't see the sense of getting up in the morning, washing your hair and hurrying to the Job Centre, because you've never known the sort of disciplines that go with a regular working life.

It takes amazingly little to lift a teenager out of the torpor of unemployment. A few days doing anything where they get paid and appreciated works wonders. When you've got a job, it's easier to find another job. And perversely, when you've got a job, you're more interested in doing other things as well. If you say, 'Why don't you read something? You always loved going through your old Blue Peter annuals' to a teenager on the dole, you will get the evil eye. And quite deservedly.

Another fundamental difference between parents who grew up in the Fifties and Sixties and their children who are teen-agers today, is the amount of violence they experience, person-ally, or in some other close, affecting way. There is, in just about every household, a television, a window on the things that are happening in Somalia and Yugoslavia that none of us can do anything about. Older teenagers tend to be less political and more cynical than their younger brothers and sisters. Nonetheless, the images are there, and if we aren't all desensitised by so much exposure to them it would be the biggest wonder. At any rate, something has deadened many teenagers to the evils of violence. Something has led them to find it acceptable, and sometimes exciting.

Fights are now a major teenage hobby. They can be personal – reasons I have heard at second hand include 'He grassed me up to my dad, right?' 'He was looking at me, right?' and 'I don't like him, right?' – or they may be tribal. Gang fights are usually to do with the way people dress, or the kind of music they follow, or simply about territory, with one street on an estate becoming a no-go area for kids from other streets. Of course fighting is as old as testosterone itself, but it used to be a last resort, especially for people articulate enough to argue, or intelligent enough to walk away. Fighting now transcends class and education. Middle-class teenagers, from good homes and good schools, go out on Saturday night prepared for trouble.

Every parent with teenagers should venture out and take a look at the pubs and clubs and streets where their children congregate. On foot. Sliding past in the Volvo is not the same thing at all. The air is thick with potential aggro. A lot of alcohol gets consumed, the noise reduces communication to grunt level, and the music is aggressive. It incites you to do something. If you're over the age of twenty-five it incites you to run away.

To breathe this atmosphere is now a normal part of teenage life, and not just for boys. Girls fight girls, girls get smacked around by boys, and girls are wildly attracted to boys who've taken a few scalps. The gangster's moll is alive and well and revising for her exams in suburbia. When I made innocent enquiries after a stabbing in a local pub, wondering out loud whether knives are now basic Saturday night equipment, I was told 'Only when they know there's going to be Big Trouble.' And how do they know? No problem. Big Trouble is usually set up, pencilled in. Word gets round and so does the excitement and fear. It begins like a ritual for letting off steam, but this is no war dance around a camp-fire. This is the real thing. Heads and kidneys get booted. Faces get rearranged. And when stories about fights get recounted, mingled with the protestations of horror there is something that makes their eyes shine. Excitement.

In the 1990s what can people do for kicks? They can't cast off in a caravel and risk sailing over the edge of the world. They can't set off to walk across Africa, because they'll bump into at least three package tours from Manchester. It is impossible nowadays to pit yourself against the elements or the fates without someone riding to your rescue, and someone else wanting to counsel you afterwards. You can live dangerously by being old, or sick or alone, but you can't have unsanitised adventures. If Dr Livingstone were alive today he'd spend his weekends bungy jumping.

Teenagers have a need for risk-taking, and an undeveloped sense of what a risk is. In your teens you do begin to have a sense of personal mortality, but you also become interested in ideas about time and space and what are we all here for. The drive to taste life gets stronger and there are none of the restraints that tame us in later years – children to rear, aged parents to care for, bills to pay. Like all skills, risk-taking is best learned by doing it, but affluent Western children are only allowed out of the nest on a long piece of string.

For some of them the answer is to improvise their thrills from what is available, chiefly drugs, crime, sex and speed – on two wheels or on four. And for some there is more than the basic human urge for living on the edge. There is a desire to get rescued. It's important that parents recognise the difference between a teenager who is feeling too swaddled, and one who is terrified of her new-found independence. Both need more practice at taking risks, but the ones who dash from one reckless venture to another need some very special support. They need to understand the paradox that they are loved and valued beyond measure, but that every safety net has a breaking point.

In all the emotional upheavals a teenager may face there are basic well-tested ways in which parents can help. No matter how wacky and off the wall a teenager may strain to be, he will still be relieved to have some regularity in his home life – meal times, house rules, jobs to do. That is not to say that Mother has to be hanging around at all hours in a flowered pinny. The kind of framework I'm talking about is achieved by thousands of busy working parents, and very effectively. It isn't knowing that dinner will be on the table at six o'clock sharp that comforts a teenager. It's knowing that at some point in the evening his parents are going to want to talk to him, preferably over a meal, and that he will be expected to help make that happen.

Of the many teenagers who have gravitated towards my fairly conventional household, the most surprising have been those raised in Bohemian style. Presented with *carte blanche* by their own parents, they tell me they rather enjoy being in a family where curfews are enforced and, barring some weighty commitment or the end of the world, everyone is expected at dinner. It seems that even great big bristly hulks with drop-dead haircuts are happier when they know that if they wander too far or push too hard they will meet a brick wall.

Parents need to demonstrate to their teenagers that there are firm limits, but also that there are safety valves. One of the most therapeutic things a disgruntled teenager or parent can do is Go Off – for a long hard walk, or a bike ride. Parents also need to encourage good risk-taking. That means saying Yes to the rock-climbing and the scuba diving. It means standing back with a sincere and cheery smile while she falls in love, or changes her mind about becoming a vet.

The most valuable thing of all that parents can give to calm the troubled teenage breast, is approval. Better than money, better than a trip to Disneyworld or the keys to the family car, approval is the thing we all crave, and teenagers especially can starve for. It's dead easy to catch your teenager doing something selfish, dangerous or anti-social. The clever thing is to catch them doing something right.

We're very ready to tell them how untidy, noisy, shiftless and unreliable they are, but to stop a teenager in his tracks and tell him you're proud of something he did seems corny and odd. If you do it, it will be received with enormous pleasure. You know how *you* feel if someone recognises that you did something brave or clever. So imagine what it must feel like, knowing that you're a lazy, pimply, uncultured slob, to be told that you did something good. Or, even better, that you *are* something good.

11 *The D Word*
Teenagers and drugs

Parents are ever fearful for their children. When the child has grown old enough to draw her retirement pension, and the parent has grown old enough to disapprove of the way she spends it, the fears are still there – of disease, or destitution, or worst of all, of death, out of turn. During our child's infancy, we shadow-box with a whole tribe of bogeymen – speeding drivers, and viruses, and teddy manufacturers who

don't fix the eyes in properly. We know our child is vulnerable
and the world is wicked, so we keep a close watch. Then
she grows up and keeps ducking round corners, out of
sight.

If there is a single subject guaranteed to strike fear in the
hearts of parents of teenagers it is the Big D, Drugs. We know
the stuff is about, in abundance. We know a lot of people
have pledged to fight a war against it, and other people keep
telling them they can't succeed. A few of us have had a close
personal encounter with a drug-related tragedy. And many of
us had even closer personal encounters with the Sixties scene.
We know enough to resist hysteria, but too much for total
calm.

We want our children to pick their way across life's mine-
field, sampling its wonders with intelligent curiosity, making
informed choices, staying healthy, and regularly changing their
underpants. We want them to be safe, whatever that may be,
and at four in the morning, when the heebie-jeebies have got
you, drugs seem the most likely threat to their safety. But is
that right? The question has to be asked.

Before making any attempt to answer it the terms of reference must be clear. When you talk about drugs what do you
mean? Something that can be injected, sniffed or swallowed?
Something illegal? Something someone else got on prescrip-
tion? Something your Auntie Joyce keeps in her sideboard?
The world is full of mind-bending substances. The way we
decide which to condemn and which to pursue with energy,
appetite and disposable income turns out to be complicated
and illogical: a synthesis of the times we live in, and the place
and, of course, of what the newspapers tell us.

I'll tell you what I mean by drugs. You may not agree. But
at least we shall know from the start how we disagree.

I mean LSD, and cocaine, and narcotics, and Speed and Ecstasy and all the amphetamine family, I mean solvents, and marijuana, and tobacco, and alcohol, and anything else that humans sniff, snort and sell the shirt off their back for. I gather them all unapologetically into the same disreputable fold because they are all substances we use to change the way we feel. It's just that some are socially acceptable and available within the law, and the others most definitely are not.

The criterion of legality is enough for many parents, and understandably. A criminal conviction is a handicap and a label that may stick for life. Teenagers don't always have the vision to see this; vision isn't very well developed in the young. So it's only right and natural that parents are desperate to steer their children far away from the taint of criminality. The problem with the law is that it isn't always easy to defend. It is a patchwork of well-tested rules, ancient, long-forgotten power struggles, and reactionary humbug. And whilst a teenager has the foresight of a flea, his powers of humbug detection are finely honed. This is why, before you embark on any kind of anti-drug crusade with your children, you have to be clear where you stand, and not just on the subject of heroin. Your Valium and your Benson & Hedges will be fair game, and so will your weekly consumption of vodka. Spontaneity can be a magical quality when dealing with teenagers, but in the matter of drugs it always pays to think hard before you speak.

Our greatest fear is that one of our children will take something and end up in a body bag. Our next greatest fear is that before that she will become one of those shadowy sub-humans we see in public health adverts, a junkie.

In our nightmares we see a black and white world of junkies and non-junkies, with nothing very apparent separating them. Mother Love, Father Love, iron discipline, cooked breakfasts, nothing promises the protection we want for our six-foot tall babies. We pour another glass, and vent our spleen on drug barons, dope fiends and the rising tide of pharmacological filth that threatens the very fabric of our civilisation. Or so it says in the Sunday papers.

It is no great comfort to know that the case in general is wildly overstated, when what concerns each of us is our own very precious little particular. But if we are to be able to talk to our children about this at all then we must have some understanding of the choices and risks they face. The Fear of God technique, so much favoured by people who hang out in those brewery-sponsored tobacco dens, public bars, does not work. And if we can't be sure of preventing our children from trying things, then we had better be sure how we can live with their experimentation, and how we can help them limit the damage.

If you allow my inclusion of alcohol and nicotine, it is hard to find any culture in the world where there is no such thing as a sanctioned social drug. Alcohol is a staple of modern Western society. Most of us see it as a vital ingredient for a congenial social life, and some eloquent minorities, the single malt buffs, and the wine connoisseurs, have invented a whole language in praise of it. There are plenty of people in the world who pity our addiction. Different places, different times. It's hard to believe, in 1992, that cigarettes used to be a badge of sophistication, and that Mr Gladstone liked a swig of laudanum before he made a speech.

When our teenagers go out for the evening most of them use something, if only occasionally, as a social prop. The four substances they are most likely to use are alcohol, tobacco, marijuana and amphetamines. The choice they make has all kinds of consequences – whether they'll be up, or down, whether they'll be fit to drive, or fit to live, and whether they're risking a criminal record. Instead of getting hysterical over the remote possibility of gutter-level heroin addiction, we have to contemplate something almost as hard, and much more likely – that our children will sample what's available and live to tell the tale.

The facts are easy to assemble. Reports on the long-term effects of alcohol and tobacco have been read by everyone, and believed by most. Pot, hash, marijuana, cannabis, whatever you call it, is well documented too, by its devoted users who praise its benign powers, and by its detractors who believe it is a short cut to the opium den. In brief, it is only mildly addictive, but it does impair judgement, and nowadays there is a lot of contaminated stuff for sale. Amphetamines and Ecstasy present a constantly shifting scene. They are the dance drugs, the designer drugs, the new names and slightly altered pharmacology that come and go on unpredictable waves of fashion. Their effects are unpredictable as well. On the night what should send you up may send you crashingly down. And in the longer term? No one has been using them long enough to know.

I recite these facts against a background hum of media panic. The newspapers are full of fighting talk from politicians, stories of personal tragedy, and awful warnings from America. Of course they are. Good news is no news. Parents do well to bear this in mind. When fear keeps them awake at night they do well to remember that thousands of teenagers try things and then move on, that thousands of people, of all ages, make regular use part of their happy, productive lives, and above all, that we are not the hapless victims of some depraved international conspiracy. We each choose our own poison, even our children, who used to play so innocently, wasn't it only yesterday?

They try things first out of curiosity. Peer pressure is a factor, but not necessarily in a coercive way. A teenager who isn't sure how to smoke a joint will be more worried about loss of face from doing it wrong than from not doing it at all. After that it becomes a question of taste, and of having the money. If they find something they enjoy, teenagers will plan and budget for it in a way that may astonish you. The daughter who never has a clean pair of tights or enough money for a taxi is perfectly capable of organising £20 worth of mind-bending substances for her rest and recreation.

We imagine our children being accosted in dark alleys; being dragged, gagged and bound into a pit of iniquity, and force-fed narcotics until their souls are no longer their own. Actually the transaction is more banal than that. They go shopping, for what they want or what they can afford, and mainly they buy from people they know. But it helps us to expiate our imagined sins – my child would not have been prey to this evil if only I had breast-fed her, sent her to a better school, been more appreciative of her finger-painting – if we have a bogeyman to hand, a Drug Baron.

In the very long run, the actions of a Colombian warlord may reverberate in your family, but railing against him is a waste of breath. Anyway, there are bogeymen much closer to home: true Brits who drink too much lager and then get behind the wheel of a car. With cocaine we all have a choice denied us by a drunken driver. We can say No.

Early campaigns against the use of illegal drugs failed to achieve their aim, which was to scare users and potential users rigid and make parents frightened to turn their backs for a moment. Teenagers, even imaginative ones, aren't good at making connections. They failed utterly to relate to the human wreckage displayed in the adverts. The occasional smoker of hash felt as remote from those images of heroin addiction as did her sherry-sipping uncle. And reasonably so. We have had dire warnings from the United States, and grim forecasts from government officials, and yet most of us go through life without knowing anyone who is destroyed by heroin.

We may also know heroin users without realising it. A carefully managed habit is not incompatible with a healthy, active life. By presenting us with the most degenerate images they could find, those campaigns made us feel comfortingly distant from it all. Shock tactics often fall wide of their mark.

This lesson was learned, and urgently, with HIV focusing our minds on a more realistic target – damage limitation. As parents, sensibly, we can only follow suit. We may long to scream 'If you ever, *ever* so much as look at a prohibited substance I shall lock you in your bedroom until you're thirty', but actually we have to let our children out, to take their exams, do their course work, and commune with their fellow creatures. So we have to master our panic. And then we have work to do in two important areas.

We have to keep track. That means being willing to listen to things we'd rather not hear. I would like my children to stay healthy, and the right side of the law, and if I could really have it all my own way, I'd like them to lead fulfilling lives without ever taking any risks. As it is, I will settle for healthy. There are some people who will never, under any circumstances, try any mind-bending substances. One or two of them might be related to me. But I work on the assumption that my children will have access to most things and personal experience of some.

It is an attractive idea that Stephen won't try stuff because he has always been such a good boy and has done his Duke of Edinburgh Silver. But then he may discover girls, or car engines, and become drawn into a new circle of friends. You may think he's fallen into bad company. And when your idea of bad company is his idea of good company, it is hard to keep talking. But you must. And with as little as possible of 'How could you . . . ' and 'Of course you realise you've broken your father's heart . . . '. You have to hold on to some neutral point of contact, where his choice of friends is not an issue, because when a disapproving silence falls, then you really do have problems.

When one of my teenagers spent the month of August huddled in the park with a crowd of deadpan Gothic posers, I radiated white-hot hostility. All those nose studs. All that sitting around in circles. Clearly it wasn't Opal Fruits they were sharing. I didn't want them in my house, or my life, but I did want to know what they were up to, and no one would tell me.

It took me a long time, years rather than months, to relax enough for anyone to feel they could tell me anything. I had to give up my All or Nothing scenario, in which my child either remains completely untouched by drugs or ends her short life with a needle in her arm. Once I eased off, the information was freely offered. Who had tried what, where they got it from, what it cost, and how they balance the accounts of risk and pleasure.

Pleasure is a very big part of the drugs picture. The main reason our children try drugs is that they're searching for pleasure, and the main reason they carry on is that they've found it. This is the other bit of hard work I mentioned. Admitting that our children aren't sick or deranged, but that they are exercising consumer choice. Unfortunately they're doing it on the wrong side of the law.

Peer pressure fills the rest of the picture. Drug-taking is woven as tightly into teenage social life as drinking is into the social lives of their parents. If they are around people who seem to have good experiences of drugs, they'll join in. If they witness something frightening, if they see someone messing up at school or losing friends, they'll respond in all the normal human ways – they'll show concern, distance themselves from anything really threatening, enjoy a little *frisson* of fear, promise themselves to be more careful, and then slip back towards their old habits. But they do make choices. That's the point.

If you suspect that your teenager is using drugs, the most important thing to remember as the waves of panic close over your head is this – experimentation doesn't always lead to addiction, but if your child does become addicted, recovery is possible.

The tell-tale signs of drug use are mainly to do with behaviour: sudden mood swings, poor concentration, disturbed sleep patterns, apathy, loss of memory, and if the addiction is an expensive one, stealing and lying. Weight loss is common too, as well as the obvious physical signs of needle-track marks, or the constant wearing of long sleeves, even in the hottest weather, to hide needle marks, and the perpetually sore, running nose of someone with a sniffing habit. The other things to watch for are the accessories of certain kinds of drug use – secret caches of little pieces of silver foil, cigarette papers, and the tiny paper envelopes that many drugs are packed in.

If it turns out that your teenager is using drugs and has problems, you have something very painful to face. On top of your fear, anger and guilt you have to accept that you have no control over what happens next. Addicts don't stop what they're doing because someone gives them a good talking to. They say they're going to stop, they make all kinds of worthless promises in exchange for attention of one kind or another – 'Give it up, and we'll buy you a car.' 'I'll never touch the stuff again.' And they always revert to their habit. An addict only stops when she personally comes to the conclusion that her addiction is bringing her more trouble and suffering than pleasure.

This is why parents who keep rushing in, trying to alleviate their teenager's suffering, can actually set her back in her attempts to recover. She has to experience the awful consequences of her addiction, including the withdrawal of parental rescue operations, before she will have the motivation to stop. In the world of rehabilitating addicts this is known as showing your child tough love. It is very aptly named.

There are all kinds of ways that families can sabotage tough loving. Buying gifts, fixing up messes, carting the addict around from expert to expert. An addict who decides she wants to stop does need help, but she has to ask for it. Then, and only then, the recovery process can begin, usually guided by experienced helpers. Withdrawal effects vary, depending on the substance. The most difficult withdrawals, the ones that need to be carried out under medical supervision, relate to substances that teenagers rarely become addicted to – barbiturates, and alcohol. Withdrawal from heroin, usually described in lurid nightmare language, is actually like a severe attack of gastric flu. The only supervision required is the kind that keeps the addict from going out and buying something to satisfy her craving.

While all this is going on it is very important that the rest of the family guard its health and sanity by maintaining a bit of emotional distance. The rest of you have to look after yourselves. Younger brothers and sisters in particular can become very neglected while someone with a drug habit is standing in the spotlight. And the stigma, real or imagined, that can make an addict's family feel socially isolated, can be put into perspective by joining a self-help group and talking to other families who know exactly what you're going through.

Allowing your child's choice-making skills to develop is one of parenthood's toughest tests. You have to relinquish things you actually long to cling to, and you have to know when to remove the safety net. It calls for consummate timing, and nerves of steel. Most of us do very well. Then, just when we think we've really let go, we realise we don't want our children making any old choice. We want them to make the choices we would have made.

You can admit this to your teenagers. In fact, you can reveal all – your idiotic fears, your justifiable fears, your worst-case fantasies in full Technicolor – as long as you say it right. If you say, 'I keep thinking you might do some LSD and have a bad trip and get scrambled egg brains and never be the same again and I really love you the way you are', that's fine because you've confined yourself to what you know and what you feel. Saying 'You're going to end up like your Uncle Jim', reveals nothing.

In the end, most teenagers who play with pills and powders give them up. They accumulate responsibilities and commitments, and confine themselves to drink and cigarettes. As young as fifteen they now have the idea that they can't really relax and enjoy themselves until they've had a drink or two. It isn't hard to see where they picked that up from.

Beer drinking is much as it used to be – done to excess by lads and by girls who want to be thought of as lads, and ending with the room spinning round. A much more worrying development is the drinking of spirits, in particular by girls in search of instant sophistication. A good preventative used to be the vile taste, but nowadays there are designer drinks that slip down so easily you don't know you've had them until you try to stand up.

The kind of drinking a child has grown up with has little influence on the evolution of his own teenage drinking. Total abstainers, discerning wine drinkers and parents who are in the pub every night all seem to produce children who go through a phase of sweet cider and British wine. Parents who have allowed their children a taste of wine at the family table find this especially galling. They had it all worked out. Introduce the child to alcohol in a safe, controlled setting. Emphasise the sensual pleasures of drinking, and play down the intoxication. And then watch with disbelief when he comes home green and legless. Risk-taking is an essential part of growing up, and alternating Uruguayan beer with Bacardi and Coke seems as good a method as any.

Of all the substances teenagers toy with, tobacco is the habit that's most likely to endure. It's legal, affordable, highly addictive, and because smokers seek the company of other smokers, becomes a currency as well as a social prop. Prevention is quite definitely better than cure, and many parents manage to keep their children off cigarettes by offering them an incentive, money, or maybe a car, if they can get to twenty-one without smoking. Very few people seem to become serious smokers after the age of twenty-one, so delaying tactics, even ones that smack of bribery, are worth a try.

For most of our children, when their teenage experiments are over and done, drug use will be limited to the occasional gin and tonic, and cigarettes for some. Every year there are five hundred times as many alcohol- and tobacco-related deaths as there are deaths related to the use of illegal drugs. When the drugs debate gets overheated, when there's talk of plagues and tidal waves and the destruction of a whole generation, we'd do well to remember that.

The Drug Scene
What things are called, and what they do

Cannabis, also known as *pot, marijuana, hash, dope, blow, ganja, grass, draw, puff, tea.*
Seen mainly as cannabis resin, which looks a bit like chocolate. Usually smoked by mixing with tobacco and rolling into a cigarette called a spliff. Can be chewed. The incidence of contaminated cannabis is increasing. Growing your own is popular but illegal.

It is mildly addictive and is the commonest first stepping stone to other drugs. Has little effect unless thoroughly inhaled, a skill which has to be acquired. Effects similar to alcohol: euphoria, impaired judgement, drowsiness. Regular users require larger and larger doses. Heavy use believed to cause chronic psychological changes. Most users smoke it only occasionally.

Amphetamines, also known as *uppers, speed, French Blues, Dexies.*
Mainly pills. Users feel euphoric, restless and invincible. It is a popular choice for all-night parties. The need for food and sleep is suppressed and so is resistance to infection. It is not *physically* addictive, but what goes up must come down. Depression, hunger and tiredness often follow amphetamine use. Regular use can lead to hallucinations and paranoia.

LSD, also known as *acid, trips, blotters, blue, smileys.*
A powerful hallucinogen. Few people try it more than once.
Usually taken from a tiny piece of blotting paper directly on
to the tongue. Also, *magic mushrooms*, which can be cooked
and eaten or steeped in water and the infusion drunk. Effects
are unpredictable and dramatic. Blood pressure, heart rate
and breathing affected, as well as altered perceptions, pleasant
or horrific. Users sometimes get *trip flashbacks* long after the
event.

Ecstasy, also known as *E*.
An amphetamine compound that acts as an hallucinogen. Pills.
Causes restlessness, *tripping*, dehydration.

Wizz
A powdered amphetamine. Can be sniffed, stirred into drinks,
or shared tongue to tongue with a kiss. Causes a dramatic *up*,
often followed by an equally dramatic *down*.

PCP, also known as *Angel Dust, Super Grass, Rocket Fuel*.
Sold as a powder or in capsules, or mixed with cannabis for
smoking. Produces a feeling of drunkenness, but also, and
unpredictably, causes numbness, delusions, paranoia, permanent memory loss, paralysis and coma.

Solvents. Also *glues, paints, aerosols*, and *lighter fuel*.
Used mainly by young teenagers. Inhaled direct from the con-
tainer or from plastic bags. Act as depressants – intoxication
followed by impaired co-ordination and judgement – and as
hallucinogens. Heavy, long-term users risk addiction. Death
by asphyxiation is a greater risk. Warning signs: smell of

solvent on breath, nose bleeds, sores around nose and mouth, weight loss.

Cocaine, also known as *coke, snow, freebase, crack.*
Produces a quick rush of euphoria followed by a rapid depression of mood. No *physical* dependence but psychological dependence sets in rapidly, making it highly addictive with doses being repeated more and more frequently to escape the *down.*

The powder is usually sniffed. Freebase is a form of cocaine that has been changed by a chemical process into a compound that can be smoked, and when smoked the effects are faster and more intense. Because of the solvents used in producing freebase there is a danger of lung damage, as well as rapid addiction. Crack is a cheaper smokable form of cocaine, which gives a fast rush and is powerfully addictive.

Other physical dangers are sudden dramatic increases and decreases in blood pressure, both of which can be fatal, paranoia, hallucinations, and if the powder is sniffed, gradual erosion of the nasal septum.

Heroin, also known as *smack, horse, H, Chinese, dragon.* When combined with cocaine it is called a *snowball.*
May be sniffed, burned and then inhaled, or injected. Produces a relaxed euphoria, and is highly addictive whichever way it is used.

Heroin is not as physically damaging as some drugs. With heroin the dangers arise mainly in two other ways. First, the need to feed the addiction takes priority over all other activities, leading to personal neglect, anti-social behaviour, and crime. Second, there is the risk of overdosing, and of HIV or hepatitis infection through sharing needles. The majority of heroin addicts eventually move on to injecting.

12 *Misunderstood, of Manchester*
Runaway teenagers

Dear Mum and Dad,

By the time you read this I'll be gone. I'm going because
    Sarah dumped me/I messed up my French oral/Nobody
understands me/I think I've caught something/I spent my
History Trip money on dynamite-strength cider.

Anyway, I just know I'm going to get grounded for ten billion years. So I'm going.

I know you love me and stuff. And Nan and Grandad and Uncle Norm and Auntie Vi. I know I'm lucky to have a Mum and Dad who let me cover up the Biggles wallpaper with Transvision Vamp. You're quite modern and everything, but there's things I can't talk to you about. Got to be. OK, you can remember acne, and where you were the day President Kennedy nearly killed you, but things are different now. There's AIDS and BSE and Chernobyl's leaking. Nothing's safe to eat. And I'm being taught maths by a needlework teacher. It's just doing my head in. I've got to get away. If I don't get away Mum'll keep tapping on my bedroom door to see if I want a mug of Horlicks.

I'm sorry if you've had to miss the Tennis Club dinner. Don't worry about me. I'll be all right.

Sam

P.S. Please ask Jessica to feed Nibbler.

*

Dear Sam,

So you've decided to run away. That's all I need. We've got redundancy notices going out on Friday, your Mum's had her veins operation cancelled again, and your Nan's started hiding things and going down the street in her nightie. And now you've run off. Brilliant.

Your mother's very upset. She won't be able to sleep for thinking of you with a needle stuck in your arm, living in Carpet City. And if she can't sleep she won't let me. Anything could happen to you. You could end up living in an underpass with a load of winos from Glasgow. Next thing, we'll turn on *World in Action* and there you'll be, starring in a documentary on begging and saying you had a rotten home life. You don't know when you're well off. When your Grandad was your age he was being shot at by the Japs.

Anyway, whatever the problem is, you should come home, get your head down, pass your exams, else how are you ever going to make anything of yourself? Me and your Mum are reasonable people. You can tell us what's on your mind. Haven't we always said 'You play ball with us and we'll play ball with you'? No sense in making things worse, distressing your Mum and everything.

All the best,

Dad

*

Dear Sam,

What your Dad is trying to say is he loves you and he wants you to come home.

Mum

*

There are three ways teenagers run away. They throw their best-loved possessions into a rucksack and slam the door on the way out, or they slip away in the middle of the night, or they just fail to come home. I have experienced all three. Each of my stories had a happy ending, and roughly the same beginning – the teenager concerned felt that she was too restricted by family rules, or that he was disapproved of, or misunderstood.

I have since discovered that the emotions I felt when one of my teenagers had run away was simply a more intense version of what I felt when one of them left home to go to an exciting new life – anxiety, powerlessness, and the restlessness and physical ache that goes with any loss.

Many runaways don't go far, and generally someone amongst their friends knows where they are likely to be. They won't necessarily tell you. The most they may be prepared to do is reassure you that your son or daughter is safe and well. But first you have to be able to contact them. For some parents this is the moment when they realise that Mozzer and Gripper, with whom their son spends his every waking hour, are just lads in black jackets. They don't know their phone numbers. They don't even know their real names. One of the most important lessons I learned from having a missing teenager was to know more about their friends, and to have a list of their telephone numbers.

As you lie awake, remembering all those documentaries you ever watched about teenagers who live in cardboard boxes, the following questions will be yomping across the moonscape of your mind – Should I call the police? Do adolescents really catch trains to London and then disappear from the face of the earth? And can my fifteen-year-old baby possibly survive without me, a hot dinner, and her priceless collection of Kylie Minogue posters? The answer to all these questions is Yes.

Calling the police may seem like taking a big step nearer to identifying a body on a mortuary slab. It's also probably going to turn out to be an embarrassing waste of overstretched crime-fighting resources. But there are two points in its favour. One is that it could get the runaway picked up off the streets and taken to a place of safety. And the other is that when he does eventually turn up, a nice chummy sergeant will deploy

the ultimate deterrent against future adventures – The Chat
That Makes You Feel One Inch Tall. Having tried it, I'm in
favour of telling the police. They *are* over-stretched, and there
isn't a lot they can do, but they are kind, and businesslike
when you are close to hysteria, and they do keep their eyes
open for missing youngsters.

There's nothing like a missing child to bring all the armchair
experts to your door. Here are a few of the missiles that
may be pointed in your direction. Working Mothers are the
principal cause of teenage vandalism, broken marriages and
international strife. Single Parents are the dry rot of civilisation. Parents who smack their children have it coming to
them. Parents who don't smack their children really have it
coming to them. Breech deliveries are trouble all their lives.
Breech deliveries born under the sign of Aries to mothers
who work and fathers who nancy around cooking dinner are
doomed to a life of Godless delinquency. Ignore this cruel
sniping. Children from the most exemplary of families crack
up, drop out, or run away.

You have time, while your teenager is missing, to number
your mistakes and misfortunes. In the cold dawn, when police
cars keep failing to pull up outside and deliver your child to
your heaving bosom, you will pace the floor and rue the day
you cruelly threw away her dummy.

A missing child plays on the family tensions nicely too. This
is a time when parents dredge up fifteen years' worth of
complaints and allegations about each other's style of
parenting. Dad says he knew there'd be trouble, letting a four-
year-old sleep in your bed because he was having nightmares
about Daleks. Dads often come out in favour of the cat-o'-
nine-tails and the school of hard knocks when they are actually
frightened and worried and desperate to know that their child

is safe. Mum says it's precisely attitudes like this that are the problem. This is often the moment when a mother will turn on her partner and tell him, possibly for the first time, that she doesn't think slurping or slouching should be indictable offences.

It is a time of raw emotion. Steam has to be let off, and not just by anxious parents. Brothers and sisters, especially younger ones, feel frightened and worried, and while the crisis continues their normal routine gets disrupted. They need to be kept informed. They still need to be cared for. And they need to feel helpful. One of the things brothers and sisters seem to find therapeutic is making preparations for the prodigal's return.

Most runaways come back. Most of them come back very soon. When they do your emotions run the whole gamut, from fury to murderous rage. Gratitude and relief come a little later. And at some point comes the inquest.

There does have to be one, I think. Running away, even if it's only for one night spent in Grandad's tool shed, is a desperate act. It means the talking has stopped. When a runaway comes home you're getting another chance. After one of our tearful, thankful homecomings I was amazed to learn what a very little thing had triggered the incident. Little to me. Big enough to persuade a fifteen-year-old to jump on the first train leaving town. He, in turn, was amazed to learn how we had all felt while he was missing. He knew, he said, that we loved him, but he hadn't expected us to take it so badly. After all, we did have three other children. And as for his sister, changing his sheets, putting a Welcome Home teddy on his pillow, and writing him a tear-stained note – you could have knocked him down with an Awayday ticket.

13 *Drawing the Line*
Teenagers and reasonable limits

It is truly amazing what some parents will endure. I've known families that have been terrorised by their teenage children, with verbal abuse or physical threats, families that have put up with stealing, free-loading, loss of privacy, wanton destruction, and menacing demands for money. Included in that sorry catalogue is my own family. So most of the solutions I propose have been road-tested personally, and some by desperate friends and acquaintances. And that is not to say each story has had a traditionally happy ending. In the complexities of parent–child relationships some of us eventually have to settle for *happier*.

My starting point is that parents have the right to safe enjoyment of their home, to privacy, courtesy and co-operation. These are all things their teenage children expect for themselves, so this is not a case of pulling rank. They are fundamental decencies that one human being might expect of another, especially in the close quarters of a family house. When teenagers neglect the rights of their parents it signals that for one reason or another they don't see them as proper human beings.

Little children think their parents are God. Slowly their eyes are opened to a more modest reality. As a teenager's eye gets drawn away by friends and heroes and the countless other grown-up role models, the image she has of her parents may slide out of focus. To her they may become two rather fuzzy figures who pay the bills and lock the door at night. Familiarity has blunted her curiosity about what kind of people they are. In her dealings with them she is literally thoughtless.

Many parents collude in this without realising what they're doing. They see themselves first and foremost as parents, and as people, only a very poor second. They trudge along, bowed down by the idea that they will be judged, always, by the way their children turn out and, if they don't turn out too well by their cheerful efficiency at clearing up the wreckage. And not surprisingly, society's blueprint for Good Parents emphasises duty, sacrifice and stoicism. Ask any parent who has had to resort to evicting a teenager, and they will tell you how little moral support they got from the world at large. Apparently, we do want parents to sort out their unruly children, but we want them to do it *nicely*.

I'm all for niceness, if it works, and firm, persistent niceness very often does. Whatever the problem I would always start with niceness. But I have learned that it has to be focused, well-prepared, and relentless. It can take months of reasonable, courteous attrition before a teenager caves in, and you are only likely to keep that up if there is something very important at stake. So first you have to know what it is you really want, and you have to be personally convinced that you are entitled to it.

Some parents are prepared to live with teenagers who never help around the house, or who leave every room they pass through looking like the ruins of Carthage. Some parents are prepared to have their property stolen, damaged, or borrowed without asking. Some teenagers are allowed to live at home, indefinitely, without studying, working, or otherwise making a move to do something with their lives. Some know that whatever trouble they get into, their parents will always bail them out. And some parents live with threats, abuse and terrifying displays of violence because the perpetrator is their own, much-loved little boy or girl, who has recently become a teenage tyrant. The amount of personal happiness parents are prepared to forgo rather than challenge their monstrous children is sad and staggering.

When you've decided what it is you want your teenager to start doing or stop doing, the first thing to do is tell them. This obvious gambit is easily bungled. Some of us find it hard to come right out and ask for what we want, whoever we're talking to. We may list all the things we don't want. We may shuffle our desires on to someone else – 'Wouldn't *you* like to know you'd always be able to find the hair mousse?' Or slide our demands in so obliquely that no one notices we've done it. There are a thousand elegant ways of failing utterly to make your point.

You should say what you want, why you feel entitled to it, and, if you can do it without playing the martyr or the despot, how you feel about not getting what you want. You have to establish a *prima facie* case that you are a reasonable person making a reasonable request. If your teenager is blind or indifferent to your rights as a fellow human, she'll ignore you or dismiss you. If that happens then the project to get her to help with the housework or to stop stealing your clothes has to be consigned to the back-burner. Your first priority is to make her see you as an individual, whose rights must be respected. But the likeliest outcome of your first statement of desire and intent is that your teenager will say 'Yeah, yeah, yeah', and then carry on regardless.

If you think the problem in your case is that your teenagers don't recognise you as an individual with rights then you should take them by storm. Shake them out of their complacent assumptions about you. Give them a rude awakening. The greyer their current view of you the easier this is to achieve. One mother I know felt compelled to pack a bag and leave home for a week. Her return was greeted with an appreciative round of applause. Another went on strike for a weekend. She slept in late, ate out, and resolutely did nothing to service the needs of her two teenage sons from Friday night till Monday morning. Her fifteen- and seventeen-year-olds were stunned and outraged. Then, when they realised she really meant it, they were amused. They told all their friends about it and basked briefly in the novelty of being poor abandoned waifs and in having an interesting mother. She says anyway that their view of her was changed by that weekend. And I roused my own teenagers to anxious fury by taking a leaf out of their book. I said I'd be home by midnight and then didn't get in till two.

If you're predictably always there, always obliging for your children, then you're probably just as predictable in the way you react to their bad behaviour. They worry you, you weep. They infuriate you, you yell. They go missing, you give chase. They can jerk you around without lifting a finger. So another way to push them off balance is to stop weeping, yelling and chasing, and go to the cinema instead.

Of course, if your teenager really depends on you for a serious emotional payout every time he misbehaves, he won't give it up that easily. Some people, and not just teenagers, make a career out of being unreliable, inconsiderate and reckless. It's easier than growing up and acting responsibly, and is also mysteriously attractive. Boys especially notice that a reputation for badness gives them a certain advantageous pull with girls. But they retain the ability to turn it off and on. They act badly around people who are impressed or appalled by it, and behave themselves at home if their parents refuse to play the game. If your teenager keeps lobbing provocative acts of badness in your direction you can undo him by allowing your return of service to deteriorate. Instead of running around, trying to outsmart him, walk away. The ability to walk calmly and deliberately away from some outrage your teenager has carefully prepared for you is one of the most useful skills a parent can acquire.

It is always easier to deal with one issue at a time. Keeping track and following through on several demands can get very complicated and tiring. Having decided what you want and having told your teenager, you then have to wait and see what happens. Usually what happens is diversionary tactics. Teenagers are expert at introducing all kinds of irrelevant arguments and sidetracks. If you don't watch out, these engage your attention, waste time, and you still don't get the dishes cleared. You have to be bloody-minded and press on with your demands. In spite of the fact that your teenager has a mountain of homework and a pulled hamstring, in spite of the fact that his friend Taff gets paid for clearing dishes and his friend Bruiser doesn't do dishes at all, in spite of the fact that you are vindictive, menopausally unhinged, and have clearly never really loved him, in spite of all of this and more, you just have to tell him, without fear or rancour, that you want the dishes cleared.

The easiest way to tell him is by calling up the stairs to where he is lurking, behind his closed bedroom door. But the only effective way to tell him is eyeball to eyeball. I am talking serious body language. When your reasonable demands are being trounced or ignored it is not appropriate to send A Stiff Note, or to begin your renewed request with 'Oh and by the way . . .' The number of times you simply repeat your demands is up to you. Some parents find it soothing to keep on and on, no threats, no diversions, just confidently repeating the request like an act of meditation. Other parents decide 'Right. I'm going to say this five times, and then I'm sending in the Marines.'

The next step is to announce what you're going to do if your request isn't met, and then do it. This is worth planning very thoroughly. Ideally your chosen form of action or inaction should specifically affect the teenager and no one else, but family life is rarely so simple. In fact, allowing other members of the family to get caught in the cross-fire can improve your chances of success. There's nothing like a bit of unrestrained peer pressure, or even peer solidarity, united in the quest for something to humour Mum and Dad, to bring about a satisfactory resolution. If there are very much younger children in the family, it may be necessary to plan your actions so that their needs aren't disregarded, but if the confrontation is between parent and teenager, with no complications, then the only precaution you have to take is to make sure that you can endure the consequences of carrying out your threat.

A few years ago some money went missing in our house. I made several calm requests for its discreet return, and at the end of the day, when none of it had reappeared and my theories about allowing thieves to make honourable amends lay dashed, I announced that without the money I wouldn't be able to buy food. 'We shall be living on bread and soup for a week,' I said, and everyone looked suitably chastened. I'm ashamed to say I wasn't as good as my word. I did have some other money, I didn't want to have soup when I could afford spaghetti, and after three days I was so bored and frustrated that I resumed normal catering and the whole matter was dropped.

Months later, more money disappeared. I repeated the twelve-hour stand-off to allow someone to own up or cough up, but no one did. My husband suggested we threaten to call in the police, but I thought our children knew us well enough to guess that we would never actually carry out that threat. I felt the best we could achieve was somehow to claim restitution for our loss. We stopped everyone's pocket money until the theft had been made good. I hoped the blatant inequity of that would shame the culprit into confessing, but it didn't. Our four children all continued to protest their innocence. As parents we didn't particularly feel any better for having taken the action we did, but at least we got the money back. And no money has ever gone missing since.

More recently I issued an ultimatum over a different misdemeanour. My children had all fallen into the habit of undressing to take a bath or a shower, dumping their clothes on the bathroom floor and leaving them there. The bathroom floor had become an intermediate clearing house for dirty laundry, temporary discards, and lightly soiled garments that were good for another wearing. And I had fallen obligingly into the role of sorter and shifter, returning things that could be salvaged to their rightful owners, and putting everything else in the washing machine. I made an announcement. I said I didn't want the bathroom littered with clothes any more. Everyone grunted and nodded, in the bathroom nothing changed, and I made the same announcement another five times. Then I said 'From today, whatever gets left on the bathroom floor will be scooped into a dustbin sack and when the sack is full it will be thrown out.'

The panic I'd predicted, with children running to rescue favourite and precious garments, didn't happen. But after I made my threatened swoop, the first sackful certainly got raided. Some items then turned up in the laundry basket. Some reappeared on my children's backs, like crumpled long-lost friends. A residue of pungent, unloved items stayed in the bottom of the sack. And then a new pile began to form on the bathroom floor.

It seems that no matter how often I repeat my performance with the sack, things will still get dropped and left. My children seem to be congenital dumpers and scatterers. But pushing it all into a sack makes *me* feel better, and when, occasionally, I reach the denouement of my threat and throw things away, I always feel calm and confident about it. So far no one has come crying to me, just too late to save a crucial T shirt.

Littering other people's space is a common thing for teenagers to do. It's anti-social and inconsiderate and it has to stop, but on the Richter scale of teenage offences it is no great shakes. Many parents live in fear of their teenager's demands and abuse, and for them it becomes a matter of great urgency to make a stand and do it successfully.

Drawing a line does not necessarily mean *doing* something, like fitting a lock on the telephone, or asking your teenager to find somewhere else to live. In some circumstances you can demonstrate that you are setting firm new limits by your inactivity, by going on strike, getting on with your own life, and refusing to play the game a moment longer. This passive technique works brilliantly with a problem like lying.

Lying takes two, at least. If no one is interested any more in whether you're telling the truth, the whole truth, or a six-pound pack of porkies, it all loses its point. Broadcasting lies into a great void is a boring business. Instead of recognising that and using it to discourage teenagers from lying, most parents tackle the problem the other way. They check stories, set up traps. And then every time they catch their child out in a lie, they reward her with wailing and wringing of hands. To a liar's cock-eyed way of thinking this then justifies another round of lies. You never believe anything she tells you, and when you do find out the truth you go berserk.

Very few lies spring forth without an invitation. Most lies are told in response to a question, sometimes because it's judged unwise to risk the truth, and sometimes simply because it's become a habit. It has to be said that some people are very hard to level with. They're so exacting, so prying, so eager and ready to tell you where you're going wrong and what you ought to do about it. The parents of teenage children are understandably liable to end up this way. More and more of a teenager's life is lived away from her parents, and she has a great need for privacy. All they can do is imagine the worst. Or ask interminable questions and wait for the lies to come rolling in.

If your teenager has become a habitual liar it is quite likely to be because you have been playing the Grand Inquisitor, waiting, coiled and expectant, for her to insult your intelligence yet again. If you stop the questions, the lies will stop. But not immediately. For a while she may actually volunteer lies: elaborate, virgin confections in anticipation of questions you have no intention of asking. Then realisation will dawn that you don't seem to give a damn. That whatever story she tells you, you greet it with the same bland politeness. From that moment on your chances of getting the truth improve by the hour.

The same kind of withdrawal can work with abusive children as well. I've known two families who suffered shocking verbal abuse from teenagers, making it impossible at times for them to make telephone calls in peace or to sit and talk to friends.

In one case, the parents agreed between themselves to ignore all threatening behaviour, and pay attention only to what was positive and reasonable in their son's behaviour. The emotional temperature dropped immediately. Their son wasn't reformed overnight. In fact he still baits them occasionally with one of his ugly threats, but they have definitely taken the wind out of his sails and, equally important, they no longer feel in a constant state of tension.

In another family the parents haven't been able to agree on a strategy and stick to it. The father favours withdrawal of attention, but the mother keeps getting hooked back in. The verbal abuse has now escalated into threats of physical violence with the mother fearing for her own life, and for the future of her tyrannical sixteen-year-old daughter.

For some parents there comes a point when the basic contract they have with their child gets abused beyond endurance. Their teenager becomes violent, or steals, or sits like a cuckoo in the nest, refusing to work or study. To decide as parents that you have gone as far as you can go is to occupy a lonely, misunderstood position. Parents are supposed to be there, whatever. Society makes no provision for parents and children to divorce one another. Ordering them to leave home evokes a shudder from kindly onlookers, who will be able to tell you exactly how thick blood should be, and how broad a parent's back. Nevertheless, being kicked out is precisely what it takes for some teenagers to see what monsters they've become.

Going away doesn't have to be for ever, although if it's an eighteen-year-old you're turfing out, she probably won't come back to live. Eighteen is a pretty good age for striking out. But younger teenagers are sometimes transformed by time away from their parents. I've seen this in a teenager sent to his grandparents, and in one who was lodged temporarily with another family. Both of them returned home with a new, mature perspective on family life.

There will be plenty of people who rush to tell you that the eleventh commandment is 'Thou shalt not oust thy teenager from the bosom of his family, no matter what liberties he taketh.' In the West we are unduly squeamish about letting our children go, no matter how objectionable they may be, until they have a career, a life partner, and the deposit for a One-Bed Starter Home. There was a time when I felt that way myself. Now, experience and inspiring examples have persuaded me that sometimes the line you have to draw is the one around the advert that says Bedsit To Let.

14 *Mittens on a String:*
The art of letting go

In the beginning was the Child. He was helpless, inarticulate, and innocent, but he had grown-ups to feed him, love him, and keep him safe. As he grew, his parents probably expanded their caring remit. They privately undertook to protect him from failure and disappointment, to bail him out, perform acts of self-sacrifice, wipe his nose, see he got a haircut, and generally guide him towards the kind of job they wouldn't be embarrassed to explain to the neighbours. The majority of parents have in mind an end product that will own a grey suit and be able to get a mortgage. Being a mime artist in the shopping precinct is something to do during a year off.

Buried in this mountain of self-inflicted parental duties are the seeds of 90 per cent of family discord – the assumption that unless you stand over your teenager with a big stick he'll never get anywhere in life. And that if he doesn't get anywhere in life, it will be damning reflection of *your* worth as a human being. What your teenager becomes is measured against your expectations, and those of the grandparents, teachers, neighbours, and anyone else who used to think he was such a nice boy.

Teenagers do make some very silly moves. It isn't surprising. They're not old enough to have had much practice at making any kind of move. But if there is one thing guaranteed to slow the learning process, and maybe discourage it for ever, it's the cry of the Greater Grey-Haired Know-It-All. 'Keith, if you stay up to watch the New Zealand Test you'll be wrecked. You'll end up doing re-takes, and then the bank won't want you.' If you are an all-seeing, all-hearing insomniac you may be able to stop your son from watching cricket in the middle of the night, but you can't police all the other routes he may take to rejection by the bank, and anyway, you will cause untold damage and delay to Keith's discovery of how much sleep he actually needs.

In certain special circumstances there may seem to be a case for parents staying very involved with what their teenagers are doing. If, for instance, you took your daughter for a paddle when she was two years old and she is now tipped for a swimming medal in the '96 Olympics, you will be expected to take an active role in her training schedule. If you bought your three-year-old a plastic banjo and he is now a potential cello soloist, his teachers and mentors will look to you to supervise his practising, and to ferry him and his cumbersome instrument from one engagement to another. Even if you didn't buy him a plastic banjo, and you personally have cloth ears and nothing stronger than a shopping trolley for transporting his cello, you will still be expected to give priority to your child's needs.

This is a very personal matter. If you see yourself as entrusted by God to nurture a unique talent, you will do everything that is asked of you, no matter what the cost to you or the rest of your family. There are no geniuses in my family so I cannot write from personal experience. But I have known a family where there was a discernible reduction of practical assistance to their musically gifted child as he moved into his late teens. For one thing, his parents were weary from years of living with a prodigy. For another, they felt that at fifteen he was mature enough to know what was at stake if he didn't practise, and to take over some of the burden of getting himself to the right place at the right time. They took the view that even geniuses have to learn how to live. Some parents would not agree. I would.

When parents try to grab control of what cannot be controlled, the consequences are dire and depressing. The teenager starts to believe she's incompetent. And her parents feel like total failures. Together they get pulled into a tight and vicious circle. The way out is to untangle all the threads of who should be responsible for what, and then let go of what doesn't belong to you. When it seems like only yesterday you were teaching her the Green Cross Code, when you're conscientious and you want the world to applaud you for your neat and studious children, handing over responsibilities is the hardest thing in the world.

Redistributing responsibilities for the things your teenager does can also be a wonderful experience. First you feel the danger, then you feel the relief. Between the two a surprise is waiting for you – that most of the things you've been trying to control aren't any of your business any more. That you could, and should, walk away from them and give your child a *real* opportunity to grow up.

Some types of teenage behaviour have repercussions mainly on the teenager herself. Taking fashion to new frontiers, losing or breaking their possessions, turning a bedroom into a pig-pen, playing truant, messing around in school, getting into trouble with the law. They are a good starting point for parents who don't believe they can let go of anything, even for a split second.

What a teenager wears is her business. Even a thirteen-year-old knows about creating impressions. She may not understand the nuances of twinsets and pearls versus the polyester budget business suit, but she certainly understands that if you wear bikers' leathers and shave your head people will not respond in the same way they would to the twinset and pearls. We dress so the world has some idea what to expect from us and, as we acquire pressing reasons to conform, we dress to show the world we understand what is required of us. Your wife may claim you permanently ruined her standing with the parish council by wearing a T shirt that said STUFF THE POLL TAX. Your mother may beg you to buy a blazer and let her die happy. But these are incidental impertinences. What you wear is your business. And what your teenagers wear is theirs.

Similarly, if a teenager opts for a life of filth and chaos, in so far as it doesn't spill into your life, let her. The kind of spillage I have in mind is where you feel you must ride to the rescue, cheque book in hand, to replace the headphones she stood on, or where you have to call in someone to exterminate the rats. Very few teenagers allow things to deteriorate as far as rats. Their squalor is self-limiting, and so, if you leave them alone with five pairs of shattered headphones, is their carelessness. All you have to do is sweat it out. You should also secure your own headphones in a place of safety.

Many mothers of teenage children pull on a decontamination suit once a week and go right on in there armed with a can of furniture polish. Some pay cleaning ladies to do it. They have more time or money than sense. What is required is a Closed Door Policy. We all need territory. Many of us go through a phase when we like to fill that territory with empty cola cans, back copies of *Playboy*, and the smell of armpit. It is a question of containment. Eventually the door opens and out of the fug there steps an adult who may buy cream rugs and fresh flowers for his first bachelor apartment.

I would allow only two exceptions to this approach (three if you include vermin). First, if you have to show teenage bedrooms to other people – builders, prospective buyers of your des. res. (but not doctors; they have strong stomachs, and anyway, environmental clues may help the diagnosis) – if circumstances dictate, I would insist that the clean-up is done by the perpetrator, if necessary at knifepoint. Second, if every teaspoon, every coffee mug, every bath towel in the house has disappeared into that stinking maw, use the same sharp knife to emphasise your demand for their immediate return. But only trespass, only go in and sort it out yourself if someone's life depends on it.

Playing truant or fooling around at school mainly affects the person who does it. You've had your education, and I've had mine. What you've achieved in life may be directly due to the fact that you did three hours' homework every night and never bunked off Technical Drawing, but for every parent like you there must be a hundred who skived and cut corners and only buckled down when they had a very powerful personal incentive.

Children who play truant in their early teens usually do it because of problems in school rather than attractions out of school. And if that is the case it *is* the parents' business. Older teenagers may also skip school because they are unhappy there, but very often they do it because they fancy a day off. My own view is, if you are satisfied that your sixteen-year-old doesn't have emotional or learning problems at school, then her truanting is more her business than yours.

It may be embarrassing and irritating to get phone calls from head teachers about your wayward child, but the main problem is your imagined loss of face. 'So! Not content with being a family that gets head lice, we have now become a family that plays truant.' Realistically you cannot supervise your teenage children's arrivals and departures at school every day, or force them to do their homework properly. Being a parent is a big enough job without volunteering for missions impossible. If your child drops out of school and then does nothing except sit around the house and strip the fridge like a cloud of locusts, *that* is your problem. You are then directly involved because you're doing all the giving, and she's doing all the taking. But for the moment I'm talking about problems that may get dressed up to look like yours, when really they're hers. Risking a future without a good History grade is a sixteen-year-old's problem, not her parent's.

If letting your teenagers take responsibility for their education is difficult, allowing them a one-to-one encounter with the forces of law and order is torment. Parents rush in with the name of a distant cousin who plays golf with the Chief Constable, anxious to expunge the smear on the family's good name. But whatever it is your child has done, he chose to do it, and short of handcuffing him to your side, you have no way of preventing him from doing it again. What may deter him is the discovery of what it feels like to be deprived of liberty, dignity and approval. A police station is a very sobering place; a courtroom even more so.

Any child over the age of ten can be charged with a crime. Until he's fourteen the prosecution has to prove his awareness that what he was doing was wrong, as well as his guilt. If a teenager is taken to a police station he can be detained there for twenty-four hours without being charged. If he's suspected of a very serious crime he can be kept there for longer. Between the ages of ten and fourteen, a parent's consent is required for fingerprinting, photography and the taking of body samples. If he's under the age of seventeen he isn't supposed to be interviewed, or to make or sign a statement, without a parent or some other non-police adult being present. And an intimate search for drugs must be carried out by a doctor or a nurse, and if the teenager is under seventeen, another adult of the same sex must be present.

Sometimes, when the police believe they have enough evidence to prosecute, they administer a caution instead. A caution avoids a prosecution, but it can only be administered if the teenager admits his guilt. The danger is that he will admit to something he didn't do to avoid going to court. Parents provide the safety net, because a caution can't be administered without their agreement, and they have the opportunity to take legal advice first.

To react promptly the first time you get a call from the

police to say they have your teenager in custody is natural. To do the same for a teenager who becomes a regular at the police station is another matter. At some point a teenager who keeps breaking the law has to be made to consider what he's going to do when he's too old for his parents to rescue him. If, instead of dropping everything and rushing to his aid, his parents take their time, and maybe let him spend a night in the cells, something important may dawn on him – that ultimately his criminal behaviour is his lookout, not theirs.

Under-seventeens are normally dealt with in juvenile court, and are usually granted bail. The pressure on parents at this point is considerable. If they or some other responsible adult doesn't attend court the trial will be adjourned until they do. If a teenager is found guilty, before he is sentenced investigations are made into his family and school background. Parents are not entitled to see the full report; only to know if some part of it relevant to them is going to be used in court.

In the case of a teenager older than fourteen the court can order that his parents be bound over to exert proper control over him, under threat of forfeiting money if they fail. The court may impose a fine and order the parents to pay it, or it may make a supervision order, which may involve the parents as well as a social worker or a probation officer. When things get to this point, parents have many obligations, and few rights.

In every family the fine detail of which responsibilities are strictly the teenager's and which belong to his parents will be different. The important thing is that the distinction is made. If it isn't, the more parents take upon themselves, the more trumped-up reasons they have to feel disappointed in their children, and the more genuine reasons they'll have, eventually, to fear for them.

When a parent is unwilling to let go, it's usually because he's concerned for his own fragile reputation. The simple matter of his son wearing mascara acquires enormous significance, rippling outwards from what Grandad will think to what the neighbours will say and then, gathering speed, to the possibility of a cancelled MCC membership, and the sabotage of a potentially brilliant career at the Min. of Ag. and Fish. Worse, it leaves the teenager with the idea that he's too incompetent even to decide what his face should look like.

If you get the message you're incompetent regularly enough, you start to act incompetent. Then the self-important parent with the grip of steel leaps up and says 'See! I said he wouldn't be able to manage his own money. This is why I always dished it out daily. This is why I wanted the Master of Trinity to have custody of his piggy bank. But does anyone listen to me?'

What was appropriate, and often essential control over your child when she was three, is completely out of place when she has become a young adult. In the main it's also impossible. Her healthiest response will be to see you in hell. While you cling to the controls she will give you a very rough ride. If you successfully deprive her of all opportunities to make decisions she may also vindicate your worst fears, flailing around, making badly judged grabs at independence.

But there is a worse possibility than that. Some teenagers don't put up a fight. They capitulate before their overbearing parents and grow into compliant adults who need someone else to make all their decisions for them. When parents say 'Fifteen's far too young for Emily to be responsible for her own behaviour', what age do they have in mind? And do they think it just happens, like your wisdom teeth coming through?

I know people drawing the old age pension who refuse to take responsibility for themselves, or who just don't know how.

You hand over the reins and they mature. That's the way it happens. Not the other way round. If you find it difficult it's because you're normal. In particular, if you have a wide spread of ages in your family, you have to keep switching back and forth between the kind of control appropriate to a seven-year-old, and the kind of trust and respect due a sixteen-year-old. That's difficult and confusing, and sometimes you're bound to mix up the scripts. Hardest of all is finding the right level for a very young teenager, who is part adult but still mainly child. A thirteen-year-old actually requires the flexible response. Before you act you have to pause and ask yourself, 'Is this Kate the young adult? Or are we dealing with the Kate who sucks her thumb in bed and still reads Famous Five books?'

The way through the difficulty of giving up control is to do it gradually, an item at a time. And not just to do it, with a tightly clenched jaw, but to take interest and maybe even pleasure in the consequences of letting go. If you insist on doing it with your head between your knees you'll miss the best part of the process – the rediscovery that your teenager is also a member of the human race. It is too easy to see a teenager as no more than a collection of vile habits. Too easy to lose sight of the unique individual who delighted you so much when she was three years old.

This approach can sound unpromising, I know. A three-year-old who insists on wearing odd socks and playing her Ralph McTell tape over and over and over again is regarded by her parents as being laudably peculiar. They recount examples of her funny little ways to anyone who'll stand still and listen. Her vulnerability makes personal quirks endearing, to her parents at any rate. Thirteen years on, her idiosyncrasies have become blemishes. In their anxiety to gain society's approval for the grand job they've made of being parents, they apply tests and standards they wouldn't dare apply to anyone else. If they did, they would be alone in the world and friendless.

Each of us lives in a world full of queer sorts who don't do things the way we do them. Sometimes it's frustrating, but mainly it's interesting. We have friends and lovers who baffle us with their methods and tastes, but we love them nonetheless. We don't meet them for lunch and say, 'Why don't you get a haircut? That girl you're seeing is going to drag you into the gutter. Have you written your Christmas thank-you letters yet? Don't slouch. You're not going to save the world by supporting Greenpeace, I hope you realise. Do you want that thing on your chin to turn into Vesuvius? Order a salad.'

If this is the kind of monologue you find yourself having with your child, there are two useful exercises you can perform. One is to think about your friends. The ones who drink too much, the ones who make one shirt last all week, and the ones who think Dorothy Squires is best played *fortissimo*. You may think you love your friends in spite of their oddities, but when you look closer you'll find it's often because of their oddities. And if you can enjoy the company of friends who do things you'd never dare to do, who aren't afraid to take risks, or look stupid, then why not the company of your growing children who do all that and more?

The second useful exercise, to be carried out inside the privacy of your own thoughts, is to remember what you were like when you were a teenager. Maturity may have added a cosmetic gloss to your recollections. Find a photograph of yourself during your most critical period of self-invention, and remember the facts. You wore flares with triangular inserts? You took a solemn vow – marriage to Mick Jagger or a life of chastity? You were never going to buy insurance or get a beer belly? You knew the questions, you had the answers. What happened?

You moved on. Maybe you now see your teens through a haze of embarrassment. A time when you looked like a joke and sounded like a twit. But wasn't there something touching and courageous about you? And can't you relate to that in your children now they've reached the age for trying to overturn the established order? If you put to one side your twenty-five years of accumulated cynicism, can't you feel delight in their energy and optimism? In the ultra-conformist bubble-packed Nineties aren't you hysterically happy to see any signs of life?

Some parents hate this approach. They know what's what. They don't like the idea of abandoning their hard-won high ground and becoming chummy with the enemy. When you are a respected member of the local Chamber of Commerce and your daughter has a perforated line tattooed round her neck, can you really afford to try empathy? Can you afford not to? The alternative is a re-run of the Battle of the Somme.

Letting go doesn't mean removing the boundaries you marked out for your children. In fact, knowing that those boundaries are firmly in place is a prerequisite to letting go. Boundary drawing is an ongoing activity, mainly during the early years of a child's life. That way, her idea of limits becomes part of her, and is very reassuring, even though she may not realise it. The better acquainted a teenager is with her parents' standards and limits, the more confidently they can stand back and let her take responsibility for her own behaviour.

As soon as parents overcome their terror of letting go, they are repaid. Do you have any idea how much energy it takes to monitor the comings and goings and secret plans of a teenager, to say nothing of whether she's getting enough vitamin C? When you hand over the responsibilities that should now be hers, that energy comes flooding back to you. And you may need it. Some teenagers don't enjoy being responsible for themselves and immediately set about behaving spectacularly badly. Of that, more later.

In many families where there have been battles over bedtimes and homework and the desirability of owning a smart jacket, the relief that follows a transfer of power is palpable. Then, when your teenager stops being a vehicle for what the neighbours expect, and what you'd do if you had your time again, she begins to emerge as an interesting individual.

I experienced this myself by noticing how I felt about other people's teenagers. When my friend's daughter dropped out of school, I sympathised with her reasons – she was obviously doing the wrong course – I feared a little for her immediate future, what with three million unemployed and a roaring recession, and then told her sincerely that I had every confidence she'd find her way. When my own daughter dropped out of college I began hyperventilating.

Observing the choices your teenager makes, from the novel position of semi-detached parenthood, is fascinating. You are reminded that there is rarely such a thing as a gold-plated failsafe Right Decision. What seems right in the short term may be daft in the long-term, and one foolish choice may lead to lessons well learned and wisdom gained. As adults we admire people who take well-judged risks, who adapt to changing circumstances, who pick themselves up, admit their mistakes, and try something different.

Lucy may well blow a potential career in insurance by listening to her radio in the middle of the night and falling asleep in Maths. She may decide against insurance anyway. Or she may discover that within reason she can stay up late *and* hold down a steady job. She may decide to become a brilliant entrepreneur who chooses her own hours and only employs people who also listen to late-night chart shows. She may become the person who makes coffee for the late-night chart show disc jockey. I refuse to attach relative values to Lucy's many possible choices, except for this – she may decide to let Mum and Dad decide, always. Without their prompting she may dither about bedtimes and careers and everything else for the rest of her life. She may never leave home. I'd definitely score that as a Wrong Decision.

Lucy could be your teenager. She could start taking responsibility for herself, aided and abetted by you. She could drop some clangers, wobble about on the edge of the nest, and then fly. Or she could be with you when she's forty, still wearing her mittens on a string, because *you* think it's for the best. That's the difference letting go can make.

15 *Lock Me Up, Tie Me Down*
The consequences of letting go

Teenagers scream and stamp and make the windows rattle with their demands that you should realise they're not children any more and get off their back. So you think about it. You go through the list of their misdemeanours, and you decide, in your wisdom and humility, to stop policing them twenty-four hours a day. You begin the frightening, exhilarating, life-transforming process of letting go. And what happens? Things get worse.

What may have looked like a simple project – turning over to your child the responsibility for getting up in the morning, becoming Chancellor of the Exchequer, not losing her hockey stick – turns out to be something much weightier. The shift in power, as good and desirable as it is, can't happen without a struggle, and there is more to the struggle than may at first be evident. A teenager needs something her parents are afraid to give: certainty. She's also afraid of getting what she needs. And if they give it to her, her parents are scared about where that leaves them. Without realising it, all of them have strong vested interests in keeping things the same.

The hot potato everyone argues about and no-one wants to handle is something called autonomy. We know we have to have it before we can make anything of our lives. Talking about it is inspiring. Fantasising about having it is exciting. Being in possession of it is terrifying. Which is why, when you get off your teenager's case and leave her to make dozens of decisions for herself, the first thing she thinks is 'Oh shit!' And that's not all. For fifteen years you've been grouching about how different your life would be if you didn't always have to be there to pick her up from Brownies and tuck her in at night. Your time has come. And your teenager isn't the only one who's thinking 'Oh shit!'

A teenager on the brink of independence, and a parent on the brink of child-free middle age, have a lot in common. Both face the adventure of choosing new directions, leaving behind what doesn't fit them any more, redefining themselves. Both are in physical and psychological turmoil. The teenager fears she may be malformed and terminally unattractive, and she knows her feet are too big. Her parent has made peace with the size of his feet, but he now has to contend with hair fall, career flop, and alarming landslides of flesh.

In families where there is a strong smell of fear, teenagers and parents collude with one another to maintain the *status quo*. They fight to deprive themselves and one another of autonomy and to see who can be the most miserable in the process. They make brief forays into the experiment of letting go, the teenager feels frightened, the parents feel redundant, and at the first sign of trouble they climb back inside the ring for a few more rounds of *If It Weren't For You* . . .

Teenagers say they want freedom, but quite naturally find it frightening once they've got it. This fear is part of the human condition. It doesn't go away on your twenty-first birthday, or when you get to be managing director. As far as we know, it doesn't go away until we stop breathing. Knowing this should help you understand why, when you ease up on a teenager very often the first thing she does is try to get you to take back control. You stop checking on whether she's going to school, and she immediately spends a week lurking in the shopping precinct chewing gum. She may just be testing your resolve. But more likely this is a cry from what's left of the little dependent child. 'Come and get me! Drag me kicking and screaming to school! I don't like being in charge of my own education. I like sulking about you being in charge of it.'

When this happens, parents move fast, especially if one of them never agreed with this newfangled letting-go business anyway. It only takes one blatant abuse of trust to send parents hurtling back to full hands-on control. Then, briefly, everyone feels better. The parents feel vindicated in their original opinion that their child is an irresponsible no-hoper, and she can carry on playing the mean and moody caged animal, which she already has the costume for, and let's face it, it is

a terrific role. The trouble starts up again soon after, and keeps recurring until a more grown-up arrangement is achieved. Round and round it goes in a dismal stagnant dialogue,
'Get out of my face!'
'Never.'
'If you don't get out of my face I'll hold my breath and then you'll be sorry.'
'Okay. We'll try it. You're on your own.'
'Free at last! Help! The cash dispenser ate my card and I need two Bs and a C for Liverpool and I don't know whether I really like drinking Black Russians. Come quick or you'll be sorry.'
'So, it seems you're not such a big girl after all. Have a cup of tea and then we'll sit down and make some nice decisions for you.'
'Get out of my face!'

The alternative, once you've taken the difficult first step towards letting go, is to persevere. Batten down the hatches, strap yourself in, and insist, no matter how much contrary evidence your teenager drops at your feet, that she *is* old enough to be responsible for herself. My own experience has been that however rough the ride, it is over much sooner if you don't dither and backtrack. Serenity and confidence are infectious. If you believe your teenager is old enough to decide about bedtimes and shop-lifting and hairstyles and sex, she'll start to believe it too. But there is nothing so morale-sapping as the massed voices of Mum, Dad, Step-Dad, Gran, Auntie Joyce, Uncle Vic and All at Number 14, whispering 'She's going to screw up. Just watch her screw up. Any minute now. There! She screwed up.'

That is not to say that if you are encouraging and quietly

confident, she won't screw up. Inevitably she will. I don't know about you, but I'm forty-five and I still screw up. The only way to keep life's slate completely free of mistakes is to do nothing. Teenagers are apprentices at judging and choosing and deciding. Until children reach adolescence they go along, on the whole, with what their parents decide. They have to. Unless they're very well endowed with the spirit of rebellion, they spend their early years believing they may be struck by a thunderbolt if they disagree, and not really daring to put it to the test.

With adolescence comes the revelation that parents are not all-knowing all-powerful hotshots. They may be weak, or ignorant, they may be poisoned by prejudice, or limited by fear. Teenagers have to find the courage to challenge those things in people they love, and very recently worshipped. When they begin they may be frightened of their own shadow. And by definition, parents can't make the problem go away. They are the problem. They have to be themselves, with their baggage of experiences and opinions, and their teenager has to dare to be herself.

What helps is having parents who are happy about who they are. Pity the teenager whose Mum or Dad still has unfinished business with their own parents. How can you weather healthy rebellion in your children if you are forty and still fighting off blue-rinsed boarding parties – 'You'll never convince me you wouldn't have been happier married to Susan.' 'Of course, I live in hopes you'll get a proper house some day. I lie awake at night and worry how they'd ever get a stretcher down that spiral staircase. Did I tell you how nice Derek's house is?'

So, having decided to Let Go, the best thing to do is let go. And the best response, as your teenager plumbs ever greater depths of fecklessness and tries to get you back playing the old games, is to do nothing. You will know if something really alarming is happening. You have been tuned to detect alarming developments since the day your child was born. If there aren't any, if the teenager concerned is just being irresponsible within the bounds of safety, refuse to notice. In most cases a teenager's fury is short-lived, and her fear subsides. She finds all kinds of perfectly sensible ways of staying healthy and achieving things, without compromising too much of her individuality. She learns how to use an alarm clock. She discovers what happens when you do all your Chemistry revision on the bus on the day of the exam. And the sky resolutely fails to fall in.

Sometimes things do go beyond the brief struggle I've described. While your teenager is going through the motions of being a useless moron and you are refusing to gallop to the rescue, other people may interfere. They may have a very good reason for wanting you to do something about your child. Her playing up may be disrupting their life or damaging their property. When this happens it's very easy to be intimidated into taking over. A teenager does something anti-social or dangerous, and up goes the cry 'Personally I blame it on the parents.' Well so do I, but not necessarily in the way these saloon bar pundits mean. A teenager of thirteen or fourteen may have been set loose too soon, or be unsure of her boundaries. But an older teenager may have failed to learn and care about the consequences of her actions because she has parents who always make excuses for her and mop up the mess.

Sometimes, when neighbours or teachers demand that you get out your big stick, it would actually be more appropriate if the teenager dealt with their complaints herself. This isn't as easy as signing a cheque to pay for damage done, or making abject apologies for something your teenager did, but can be very worthwhile. Feeling the full blast of someone else's complaints can have dramatic improving effects on the teenager. You may earn a passing reputation as an irresponsible parent, but it is worth it to get more responsible behaviour from your teenager.

It also happens occasionally that a teenager doesn't settle down when she realises you meant what you said about letting go. In quite fundamental ways she can't or won't accept her new responsibilities and freedom, and goes to dangerous lengths to get you to supervise her again. As parents each of us has our limits. There is only a certain amount of anxiety we can absorb before our own health suffers and we deprive other members of the family of the time and energy they are entitled to. The first thing to remember is that most teenagers who go to the brink of what's legal, what's safe or what's decent and threaten to jump, are neither sick nor evil. They are just highly skilled at jerking you around until they get the kind of attention they crave.

I do not underestimate how terrifying threats made by a child can be, especially when that child stands head and shoulders above you. The earlier you resolve to deal with this, the better your chances of succeeding by simple withdrawal. When a young teenager makes threats, if you become studiedly thick and unobservant instead of hitting the panic button, she will soon get discouraged. A threat that goes unacknowledged falls completely flat. But if your teenager learns that you are responsive to threats, by the time she has grown taller than you simple withdrawal of attention may not be enough. Having experienced demands made at knifepoint, I know the terror and impotence that paralyse normal thought processes. In her frustration my teenager threw the knife, just as the rest of the family got clear of the room. I did two things. Three, if trembling counts as doing. I refused to give in to her demands. And I hid the sharp knives for a few days, until the air was cleared. The incident has never been repeated.

When a teenager acts bad, mad or plain infantile there are two things you can do, depending on her age, the gravity of the situation, and on your own strengths and weaknesses. You can tell your teenager exactly what you think and how you feel. 'I hear you were so drunk last Saturday you couldn't stand up. I can't follow you everywhere and stop you drinking so much. You're old enough to decide things like that for yourself. But when I hear about it I imagine you ending up on a park bench with a pickled brain and no family to go home to. I have nightmares about it.' It's important that you don't miss out the bits about knowing she can take care of herself if she chooses to. That way you let her know that you're sticking to your guns in spite of your anguish. Alternatively, you can ask for outside help.

Some parents will go to very great lengths to contain and solve a problem within the privacy of the family. But in an emergency, having established that something has to be done, it pays to be open-minded about who should do it. When a teenager's refusal to take responsibility for herself leads her to dangerous extremes someone, a policeman or a doctor for example, may have to draw the line for her. Ideally, those kind of external controls should be applied for as short a time as possible, so they must be effective and on target. And while some figure of authority is setting firm, temporary limits for a teenager, her parents need to stay committed to the idea that she is capable of growing up, and make sure she knows that's what they believe. If she can see you, waiting in the wings with a fire extinguisher and a box of sticking plasters, her reasons for shaping up immediately dwindle.

The teenager who demands freedom and doesn't like it when she gets it is only half of the story. What she is being asked to take on, her parents are being asked to give up, and that can be painful. If keeping Melanie on the straight and narrow has been your *raison d'être* for fifteen years, what is to become of you now? As parents we should not underestimate the effect of looming redundancy. While we are making all the right noises about enjoying new-found freedoms, we may be quietly applying the brakes because we don't want to be too free too soon. Any parent who has been involved in caring for his children gets these feelings. If there have been nannies and schoolmasters and long separations the effect is diluted by time and habit, but every parent eventually has to ask himself this question 'If I am not Melanie's caretaker, what am I?' In the Nineties, when the finger of Equal Opportunity has reached out and touched redundancy, Mum still has a harder time with this than Dad.

Dad may have looked forward to the day when he can plan a week's fishing on Speyside without considering school holidays, the cost, and the fact that Melanie can't sit still anywhere for five minutes without needing a Pepsi and the promise of seeing a *Police Academy* movie. When he finds he can actually go fishing without a backward glance he may sink briefly into a depression, leafing through photograph albums of Melanie aged five. Very soon he will be on the mend, packing his rods, and giving thanks that his daughter is now so absorbed in the pursuit of a zit-free chin and a boy called Jason that she won't even notice her Dad's gone. For Melanie's Mum the story is much more complicated.

The mothers of today's teenagers work for a living. Very few of them are in the boardroom. Most of them do work of mind-numbing futility, and they do it because it's the only way their families will be fed and housed. Career plans and schemes for education and personal development straggle far behind the first priorities of these women, which are to hang on to their jobs and keep the home fires burning.

Years ago, when mothers stayed at home with flour in their hair and a duster in their hand, they pounced on each arrival before he'd even had time to throw his satchel across the floor. 'You're late. Look at your trousers. Don't eat that, you'll spoil your tea. Get your viola out. What did Mr Robinson say about your maths? You're going to have a bath tonight.' It is a wonder any of us ever grew up. I suppose we did it by blocking out the machine-gun rattle of Mum in full flood, secretly eating things that would spoil our tea and working out ways to not do viola practice. When we did grow up we could see Mum's game more clearly. She had been nagging and wheedling us into a state of submission and dependence so as to keep herself in a job.

The contrast between mothers who elaborated housewifery into something that consumed all the hours in a day, and today's mothers, is startling. Today's mother is always four hours short. She runs from the clocking-out machine to the supermarket, from the supermarket to the ironing board, and sometimes she fits in a Parents' Evening as well. Clearly she is not under-employed. Clearly mothers today must welcome the opportunity to hand over some of their responsibilities – choosing their children's clothes, supervising their children's homework, launching seek-and-destroy operations against the smell in their son's bedroom, worrying about their daughter's sex life. Clearly.

Well actually it hasn't worked that way. Today's over-burdened harassed working mothers would love to hand over all kinds of things, but *not* the position of Indispensable

Numero Uno. Mothers who work in shops and offices and factories know that out there they still don't amount to much. They are numbers on a payroll, names on a coffee rota. Their power base is at home.

Being a guiding light to your children is a very hard thing to give up. Whether you do the kind of work where you frankly have no power, or the kind of work where you merit a reserved space in the management car park, there is truly nothing so intoxicating as playing the domestic supremo. When we let go of responsibilities that rightly belong to our teenage children, what is left for us? A few more paydays? Another rung or two climbed on a corporate ladder to nowhere? Long empty evenings yawning before us, with no one needing to be nagged or cuddled or picked up from the disco at eleven? In allowing our teenagers to grow up we suffer a profound loss.

But we have to do it, and it's vital for the independence of our children that we do it genuinely, not watching for the slightest stumble so we can rush to pick them up, not wearing an expression of tortured anguish. The more absorbed we are in our own lives, the more convincing we are when we tell our children to get on with theirs.

Having interests and passions separate to our role as parents, and being willing, increasingly, to put those interests first, is the key to properly letting go. If we really want teenagers to develop a strong sense of self, we have to set them an example. Protesting that you can't possibly build a greenhouse or sail the Atlantic until your children are safely married is not an inspiring way to behave. It reeks of cowardice. And it garbles the message that you have better things to do with your life than supervise a six-foot youth with designer stubble.

I have worked this angle very hard. Not only have I insisted that I have a life of my own, I have also used it as a kind of sheet anchor whenever my older teenagers try to lure me back into sorting out their lives. When one of them puts on an Oscar-winning performance, standing outside my door ruining his life loud enough to get me *really* worried, I no longer tut or sob. I cast a quick eye over the situation and if it looks like a try-on, and it often does, I walk away. If I can, I do something nice. Something for me.

The temptation to be a fount of wisdom, money and brilliant rescue plans is great, but I have decided to try and resist. I have decided to accept the downs and ups of life with four trainee adults, and resign from my position as a one-woman crash squad. Any day now.

16 *Smiling Through*
The good news about teenagers

Your children won't be teenagers for long. At the very worst, if one of them makes a premature start at the age of twelve and drags it out, mooning around the house and dripping tea bags everywhere until he's twenty, that's still only eight years. A mere drop in the ocean of your lifetime. And most children only spend about half that long being seriously difficult and objectionable. Anyway, it isn't all bad news. There are many ways in which life with a teenager is exciting, interesting, even pleasant. You probably just need reminding what they are.

The teens are the first time you get a glimpse of the adult your child will become. Some people have children because they want an excuse to buy one of those prams that converts into a pushchair, baby bouncer, and twelve-speed mountain bike. Or because they love squidgy, dribbly little faces snuffling on the shoulder of their cashmere cardigan. But after the honeymoon there has to be some greater purpose to sustain us through the years of parenthood, and most of us would express it in terms of launching a bit of ourselves out into the great unknown of posterity. Try as we might, we can't make our children exactly like us, but there are usually enough similarities to satisfy the appetite we all have for immortality.

A teenager may look like you, and even sound like you, but she's much more interesting than a clone. She has her own thoughts and tastes and opinions, and some of them may truly amaze you. Teenagers are idealists and optimists. They have the courage of innocence. Their bodies are strong and beautiful. And they are almost completely free of bullshit.

One of the most wonderful things about having a teenager in the family is their discovery of things you'd forgotten or just never noticed. They are a fresh pair of eyes on the world, and it's worth giving a second thought to their new enthusiasms and causes. Their process of discovery could be your chance of rediscovery. Another wonderful thing is that you can talk to them. From time to time teenagers can be persuaded to abandon the silly voices and the Neanderthal grunts, and really talk. You can sit down with a jug of coffee or a bottle of wine, and discuss something, especially something philosophical, without having to read them a Milly-Molly-Mandy story or fix the arm back on Tina Tiny Tears.

Teenagers are like slightly peculiar new acquaintances. You think you may be going to like them, and at any rate you find them engaging enough to put up with their eccentricities and get to know them better. If you are patient and willing they could become friends for life. And they, in turn, have friends of their own, all evolving into a kaleidoscope of interesting young adults. Remember the days when having his friends round meant covering the soft furnishings with sheet polythene, and setting the kitchen pinger to go off every half-hour to remind you to ask little Barney if he wanted a wee? Isn't life pleasanter now that little Barney has become big Barney and has dropped by to tell you all about learning to abseil in Derbyshire?

There are so many things you can do with a teenager. You can watch grown-up television programmes and films together, and talk about them afterwards. You can let him design his own bedroom, or cook you dinner. You can borrow her books and magazines, or her clothes, if you really want to. *You* can use *her* shower gel. You can get him to help you shift a wardrobe, or paint a ceiling, or explain how a fax machine works. You can watch her talking to her sister without pinching her crisps or stealing her tricycle. You can ask him to lend you a fiver till Friday, and you can take him for a long walk around Venice without once having to give him a piggyback ride.

And then there are the welcome liberations. You can get rid of the doll's house and the Darth Vader laser wand. You can give up cutting her toenails, and you can finally come clean with him about Father Christmas, Easter Bunny and the Tooth Fairy. You can let go of your dreams about your son dancing at Sadlers Wells, and your daughter playing for Yorkshire, or was it the other way round? It doesn't matter.

The thing about children is, they always have a history that includes you. In the beginning you and your children were connected by the customs and traditions that were yours to share and pass on. Now you have an extra dimension to your mutual history, because your teenager will be starting to create customs and traditions of his own. That's what keeps a family dynamic and alive. You have to bear that in mind in those dark hours when all you can think is that you've got a sixteen-year-old who wears black eyeliner and failed Religious Knowledge, and maybe you should have sent him to Gordonstoun after all. If it weren't for all this diverse evolution your family tree would just read:

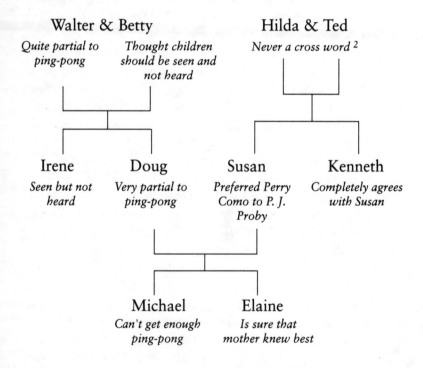

Walter & Betty
Quite partial to ping-pong
Thought children should be seen and not heard

Hilda & Ted
Never a cross word [2]

Irene
Seen but not heard

Doug
Very partial to ping-pong

Susan
Preferred Perry Como to P. J. Proby

Kenneth
Completely agrees with Susan

Michael
Can't get enough ping-pong

Elaine
Is sure that mother knew best

When you have a teenager in the house you have a view-finder pointed towards a future that you will not be at liberty to visit personally. Your son with the eyeliner, who believes human beings would be a lot kinder to one another if they stopped eating factory-farmed chickens, and your daughter, who wants to be a free spirit, save the ozone layer, and have a nice detached house with festoon blinds, these are your emissaries to the twenty-first century. If that doesn't sustain you through late nights, weird clothes, missed periods and all the rest, if that doesn't interest you or excite you, even ever so slightly, then you might as well be dead.

Advice and Support for Teenagers and Their Parents

UNITED KINGDOM

Alcohol Abuse
Alcohol Concern	071-833-3471
Alateen	071-403-0888
The Accept Clinic	071-385-2451

Drug Abuse
Families Anonymous	071-431-3537
Release	071-603-8654
ADFAM National	071-823-9313
National Campaign against Solvent Abuse	081-733-7330

Eating Disorders
Eating Disorders Association	0494-521431
Anorexia & Bulimia Association	081-885-3936

Gambling
Gamblers Anonymous	071-352-3060

Pregnancy
British Pregnancy Advisory Service	071-222-0985
Pregnancy Advisory Service	071-637-8962
Ulster Pregnancy Advisory Service	0232-381345

Homosexuality
Gay Switchboard   071-837-7324
Acceptance Helpline for Parents   0795-661463

Rape
Rape Crisis Centre   071-278-3956, and many local centres

HIV & AIDS
National AIDS Helpline   0800-567123
Terrence Higgins Trust   071-242-1010
Body Positive   071-373-9124

Cults
Family Action, Information & Rescue   071-539-3940

Missing Persons
Missing Persons Bureau   071-387-2772
Suzy Lamplugh Missing Persons Helpline   081-392-2000

General Counselling
Institute of Family Therapy   071-935-1651
Samaritans   local numbers nationwide

AUSTRALIA
Use local phone listings. If the organisation is not based in
your local area, please ring its office in your state's capital,
and they will direct you to the relevant telephone number.

Alcohol Abuse & Drug Abuse
Alcoholics Anonymous
Alcohol & Drug Information Service
Narcotics Anonymous

Eating Disorders
Anorexia Nervosa Society
Overeaters Anonymous

Gambling
Gamblers Anonymous
Lifeline

Pregnancy
Childbirth Education Association
Pregnancy Support Centre

Homosexuality
Gay Crisis Network
Gay Counselling Service

Rape
Rape Crisis Centre
Lifeline

HIV & AIDS
AIDS Council
Quest for Life Foundation

Cults
Centacare

Missing Persons
Red Cross
Salvation Army

General Counselling
Lifeline
Community Health Centre

NEW ZEALAND

Alcohol Abuse
Alcoholics Anonymous: Refer local office
Alcohol & Drug Dependency
Service/Centre: Refer local office

Drug Abuse
Narcotics Anonymous: Refer local office
Odyssey House Drug Rehab Centre:
  Auckland: 390 Mt Eden Rd   09-623-0228
  Christchurch: 98 Greers Road   03-358-7791

Pregnancy
Pregnancy Help:
  National Office: PO Box 12 000 Wellington
Pregnancy Counselling Services:
  PO Box 33423 Takapuna Auckland 09-489-6505

Homosexuality
Gayline: 09-303-3584

Rape
Rape Crisis Centres:
  PO Box 6181 TeAro Wellington 04-384-7028

HIV & Aids
NZ Aids Foundation:
    PO Box 6663   09-303-3124
    Wellesley Street   Auckland

Missing Persons
Missing Persons Bureau: Refer local police

General Counselling
Anglican Trust for Women & Children:
    National Office   09-276-3729
    PO Box 22363   Otahuhu   Auckland
Justice Department: Refer local office
Lifeline: Refer local office
Pacific Island Youth Development:
    PO Box 21068   09-837-2558
    Henderson   Auckland
Special Education Services:
    National Office   04-499-2599
    PO Box 10601   Wellington
Youthlink Family Centre:
    National Office   PO Box 9846   09-309-4484
    Newmarket   Auckland
Outward Bound Trust of NZ:
    National Office   09-379-2356
    PO Box 3459   Auckland
Youthtown (formerly Boystown):
    PO Box 5899   Auckland   09-379-5430
Presbyterian Support Services:
    National Office   PO Box 9079   04-801-6005
    Wellington

Department of Social Welfare: Refer local office
Youthline Counselling Services:
  PO Box 9300 Newmarket Auckland 09-379-8996
Barnardo's New Zealand:
  66 Dixon Street   04-857-560
  PO Box 6434 Wellington
Marriage Guidance New Zealand:
  National Office   04-472-8798
  PO Box 2729 Wellington
Methodist Mission Family Services:
  National Office   03-666-049
  PO Box 931 Christchurch
Department of Health: Refer local office
Home & Family Support:
  344 Mt Eden Road   09-608-961
  Mt Eden Auckland
Samaritans:
  PO Box 1200 Wellington   04-473-9739
Toughlove:
  31 Uxbridge Road   09-534-7022
  Howick Auckland

CANADA

General
Kid's Help Phone 1-800-668-6868 National, bilingual
24-hour helpline for kids and teens. They maintain a national
database of services and will refer callers to the appropriate
agency in their area.

Big Sisters & Big Brothers will often assist a parent or teen in finding appropriate services locally, as well as matching children up to 18 with volunteers who serve as role models/companions for teens of single parents.

Council for Exceptional Children
#750, 2 Robert Speck Parkway, Missisauga 242 1198
416-897-9756   Fax 416-279-0911

Family and Children's Services (or its equivalent in provinces other than Ontario) will have reference to services in each city or region. These may include:
Human Rights and Anti-Racism
Environmental Concerns
Sexual Abuse or Incest
Sexual Harassment or Labour Concerns

Alcohol Abuse
Al-Anon: counselling and groups for family members of alcoholics
and
Ala-teen: counselling and groups for teens with alcohol problems
Both are listed in the telephone book in each city or town where there is a group meeting.

Drug Abuse
Addiction Research Foundation (ARF) in Ontario
1-800-463-6273 information only
Ministry of Health Ontario: 1-800-567 Drug counselling
Narcotics Anonymous listed in telephone directory where available

Eating Disorders
Overeaters Anonymous: Self-help for anorexics and bulimics.
Listed locally or write to:
Christchurch/Deerpark
1570 Yonge St
Toronto Ontario.

Gambling
Gamblers Anonymous
As with other 'Anonymous' organisations, local telephone
listings indicate the existence of a local chapter.

Pregnancy and Abortion
Birthright-counselling on pregnancy only 1-416 469-4111
Or write to:
777 Coxwell Ave
Toronto Ontario
M4C 3C6

Planned Parenthood
Promotes healthy sexuality, birth planning, freedom of
choice in pregnancy decisions
#430, One Nicholas St
Ottawa Ontario
also local chapters
613-238-4474 Fax 613-238-1162

Homosexuality
Lesbian and Gay Youth Toronto Phoneline: peer counselling
1-416-964-1916/voice 1-416-964-3201/TTD
Parents and friends of Lesbians and Gays
(PFLAG) – support group 1-416-457-4570

Rape Crisis, Sexual Abuse, Incest
Local Sexual Assault Support Centres often are not set up
to deal with clients under 18, but will have referral numbers
for appropriate services in your area.
The Federal Department of Justice has publications (eg 'What
to Do When a Child Tells You of Sexual Abuse') some
geared to the babysitter or other teen, write to:
Communications and Public Affairs 1-613-957-4222
Department of Justice
Ottawa Ontario.
K1N 0HB

HIV & AIDS
Local AIDS Committee
or
In Ontario: AIDS Hotline 1-800-668-AIDS
In French: 1-800-267-SIDA
National AIDS Clearing House information line
1-613-725-3769

Suicide Prevention for teens
Local crisis lines

Missing Persons
Childfind (helps to locate missing children) 1-800-387-7962
Parentfinders (helps to locate parents) 1-416-486-8346

SOUTH AFRICA

Alcohol Abuse
Alateen   011-337-4486
Alcoholics Anonymous   011-836-8735

SANCA   011-836-5942

Drug Abuse
As above

Eating Disorders
Tara   011-783-2010

Pregnancy
Pregnancy Crisis Line   011-614-3149
Termination of pregnancy 011-488-4120
NCEPA   02281-44013

Homosexuality
Gay advice bureau 011-643-2311

Rape
Emergency 011-393-1020 code 7125
Lifeline   011-728-1347
POWA   011-642-4347

HIV & AIDS
AIDS Hotline 011-725-6710
Community AIDS information & support centre
011-725-6712

General Counselling
Childline   0800-123321
Child Protection Unit   011-477-1390
                             021-45-3697
                             031-23-1101

                                           012-325-1800
                                           041-54-7916
                                           051-30-3351
Institute of Family Therapy, FAMSA   011-833-2057

Index